A Look into Space

A Look

into space

A Supplement to Childcraft—The How and Why Library

World Book, Inc.
a Scott Fetzer company
Chicago London Sydney Toronto

World Book, Inc.
525 W. Monroe
Chicago, IL 60661

ISBN 0-7166-0694-1
Library of Congress Catalog Card No. 65-25105
Printed in the United States of America

1 2 3 4 5 6 7 8 9 10 99 98 97 96 95 94

Contents

Touring the Universe 150

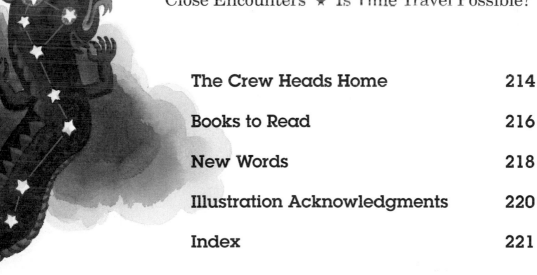

Living in the Space Age 180

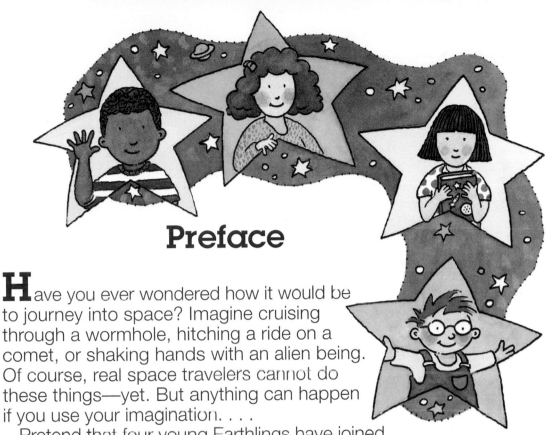

Preface

Have you ever wondered how it would be to journey into space? Imagine cruising through a wormhole, hitching a ride on a comet, or shaking hands with an alien being. Of course, real space travelers cannot do these things—yet. But anything can happen if you use your imagination. . . .

Pretend that four young Earthlings have joined Major Vox, a scientist from a faraway planet, on a tour of the universe. On their journey, Major Vox will teach them all about real-life space. They will learn about the planets, the sun, the stars, galaxies, and more. They will see what it truly means to live in the space age. And they will do it all aboard the make-believe star cruiser SpacePod.

Who are these lucky Earthlings? First there is Ben, the oldest. He's wild about machines, and SpacePod was too cool to miss. Suki is a science-fiction bookworm. Annabelle is a math and science whiz. And finally there is Little Rollo, a bit of a mischief-maker. Major Vox may have his hands full with this guy.

The gang is ready for lift-off. Are you? Come along and see what space adventures await this fearless bunch. To keep up with their journey, turn to the first two pages of each chapter. Blast off!

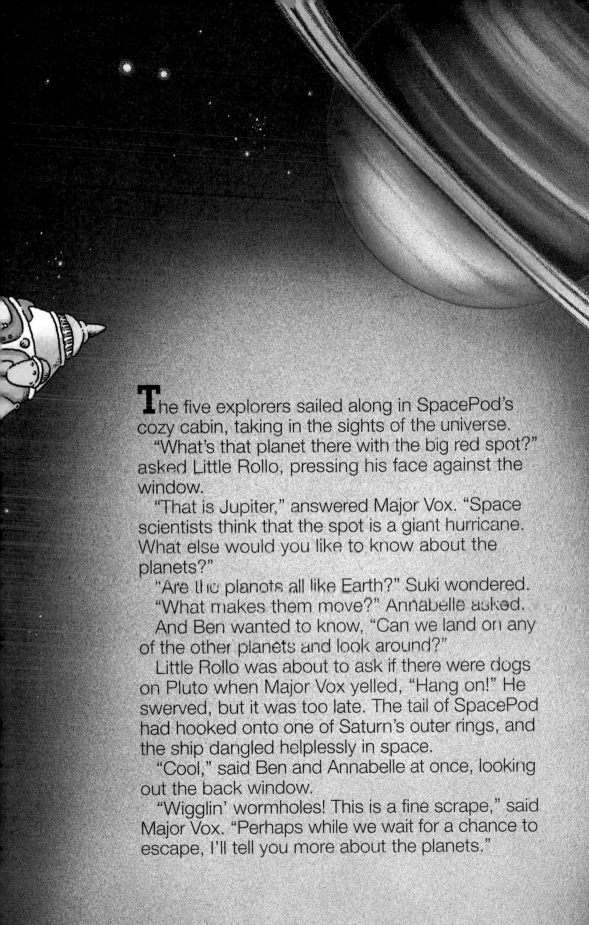

The five explorers sailed along in SpacePod's cozy cabin, taking in the sights of the universe.

"What's that planet there with the big red spot?" asked Little Rollo, pressing his face against the window.

"That is Jupiter," answered Major Vox. "Space scientists think that the spot is a giant hurricane. What else would you like to know about the planets?"

"Are the planets all like Earth?" Suki wondered.

"What makes them move?" Annabelle asked.

And Ben wanted to know, "Can we land on any of the other planets and look around?"

Little Rollo was about to ask if there were dogs on Pluto when Major Vox yelled, "Hang on!" He swerved, but it was too late. The tail of SpacePod had hooked onto one of Saturn's outer rings, and the ship dangled helplessly in space.

"Cool," said Ben and Annabelle at once, looking out the back window.

"Wigglin' wormholes! This is a fine scrape," said Major Vox. "Perhaps while we wait for a chance to escape, I'll tell you more about the planets."

Planets: The Namesakes of the Gods

Mythology is a collection of old stories from a certain region, culture, or country.

Once upon a time, the gods of Roman and Greek mythology gathered for dinner. After dessert they loosened their togas, relaxed, and shared stories of times gone by. Soon the discussion turned to their namesakes—the planets.

"My planet is a chip off the old block," bragged Mercury, speediest of the gods. "Mercury travels around the sun at 108,000 miles (174,000 kilometers) per hour—faster than any other planet—and completes its orbit in just 88 Earthdays.

As you all know, the time it takes a planet to go around the sun equals its year. So that means Mercury has the shortest year in the solar system. Earth takes much longer—365 days—to go around the sun."

Jupiter, king of the gods, didn't like it when his son Mercury boasted. "But your planet also has one of the longest days in the solar system," he pointed out. "A day on Mercury lasts two of its years—176 Earthdays to be exact.

Orbit is the path of a body in space, such as a planet or moon, around another body in space.

The **solar system** is made up of the sun and the planets and other heavenly bodies that travel around the sun.

Mercury

"A day on the planet Jupiter, on the other hand, lasts less than 10 hours. No other planet can beat that time.

"What's more, Jupiter is larger than any other planet. Why, it's wider than 11 Earths lined up in a row! And it weighs more than all the planets put together."

"That's a lot of gas," Mercury said.

"What was that?!" Jupiter boomed.

"Your highness, I was just saying that the planet Jupiter consists mostly of gas."

"So?" Jupiter replied.

"So…Jupiter may outweigh Mercury, but cup for cup, the iron and rock that make up Mercury are heavier than the gas on Jupiter."

"Mercury, you talk as if your planet were special," chuckled Saturn, the father of Jupiter and the god of farming. "Did you know that one of my planet's moons, called Titan, is wider than the planet Mercury? In fact, rumor has it that Mercury may have started out as a moon of Venus."

Mercury blushed from the tips of his head wings to the tips of his heel wings.

"Scientists just toy with that idea," Pluto, the god of the underworld, said. "They say similar things about my planet. Frankly, I think Pluto is special because

Saturn

it is the smallest planet and takes the longest to travel around the sun—248 Earth-years to be exact." The other gods looked at one another and smirked.

"My planet's cloak of creamy clouds reflects sunlight almost like a mirror," cooed Venus, goddess of love and beauty. "Venus shines so bright, people call it the morning *and* evening star. What can compare with that?"

"Saturn's rings, of course," Saturn replied. "Dark rings made up of dust or rock may circle Jupiter, Uranus, and Neptune, but *seven* rings made up of thousands of narrow, icy ringlets circle Saturn. And they all shine bright."

"My planet is more than just bright; it's blue," Neptune, the god of the sea, spoke up. "The frozen methane that surrounds Neptune gives my planet this beautiful color."

"I prefer the orange-red glow of my namesake," piped up Mars, the god of war. "Mars's color comes from iron-rich dust that powerful dust storms stir up."

"If any planet is worthy of note, it's mine," added Uranus, the Greek god of the sky. "What other planet rotates on its side?"

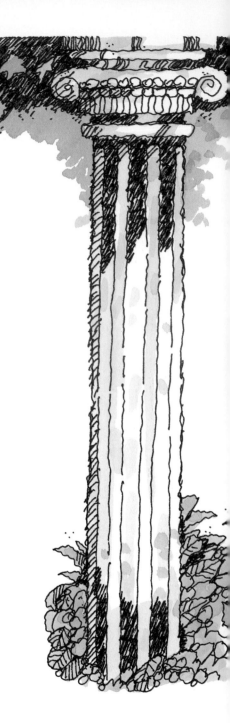

NEPTUNE

MARS

"Mine rotates backward," Venus quickly replied. "So, on Venus the sun rises in the west and sets in the east. Nothing can top that."

Mother Earth, fed up with the planets' boasting and arguing, cleared her throat and declared, "Without a doubt, Earth ranks as the most special planet."

"What? It's surely not the largest planet," Jupiter blustered.

"Or the brightest," Venus sniffed.

"Or the quickest," Mercury added.

Mother Earth smiled and replied, "But only Earth has water, air to breathe, and a comfortable temperature. These things make it possible for plants, animals, and human beings to live there. And after all, humans named the planets, making them your namesakes."

The Roman gods couldn't argue with Mother Earth's point. All at once, they raised a cheer to humans' cleverness and good taste. Then they said their good nights and headed home.

Make a Solar System Mobile

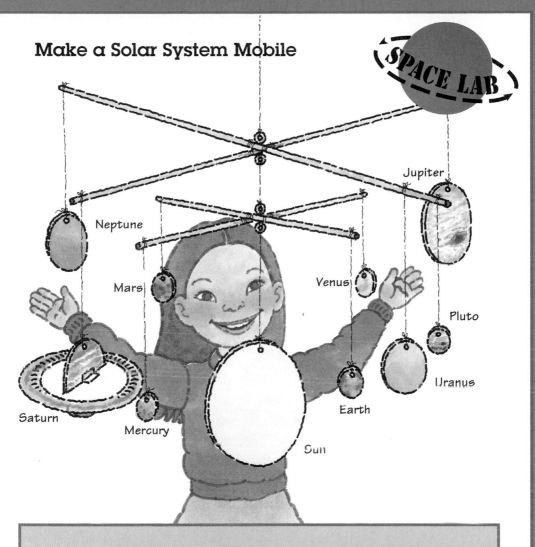

Things you need:

- 4 dowel rods, 1/8 in. (.3 cm) in diameter:
  one 17 in. (43 cm) long
  one 21 in. (53 cm) long
  one 35 in. (89 cm) long
  one 43 in. (109 cm) long
- a spool of "invisible" nylon thread
- 4 rings, 3/4 in. (2 cm) in diameter
- crayons or markers
- a large piece of white posterboard
- compass*
- scissors
- glue
- tape
- hole punch
- yardstick or meter stick
- large paper plate

*Ask a grown-up to help you if you don't know how to use a compass.

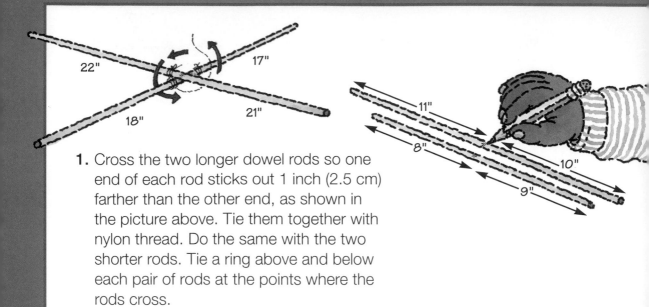

1. Cross the two longer dowel rods so one end of each rod sticks out 1 inch (2.5 cm) farther than the other end, as shown in the picture above. Tie them together with nylon thread. Do the same with the two shorter rods. Tie a ring above and below each pair of rods at the points where the rods cross.

2. Cut an 8-in. (20-cm) piece of nylon thread. Tie one end of the thread to the ring below the longer rods and the other end to the ring on top of the shorter rods. Leave 6 in. (15 cm) of thread between the rings.

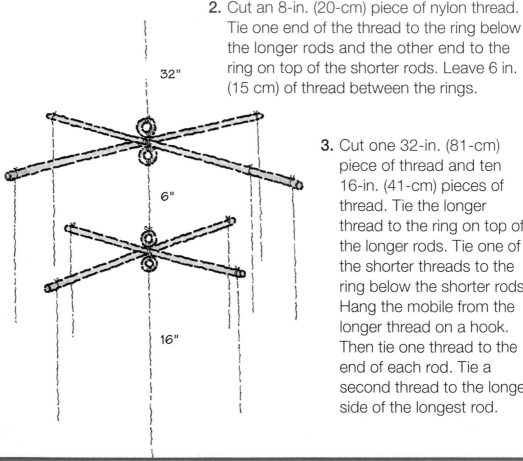

3. Cut one 32-in. (81-cm) piece of thread and ten 16-in. (41-cm) pieces of thread. Tie the longer thread to the ring on top of the longer rods. Tie one of the shorter threads to the ring below the shorter rods. Hang the mobile from the longer thread on a hook. Then tie one thread to the end of each rod. Tie a second thread to the longer side of the longest rod.

4. To make the planets and the sun, draw 11 circles on the posterboard using a compass. Set your compass to the following radii:

Sun, 4-1/2 in. (11.5 cm)
Jupiter, 3-3/4 in. (9.5 cm)
Saturn, 3-1/4 in. (8.5 cm)
Neptune, 2-1/2 in. (6.5 cm)
Uranus, 2-1/4 in. (6 cm)
Earth, 1-1/2 in. (4 cm)
Venus, 1-1/4 in. (3.5 cm)
Mars, 1-1/8 in. (3 cm)
Mercury, 1 in. (2.5 cm)—make two
Pluto, 3/4 in. (2 cm)

Cut out and label each circle. Glue the two Mercurys back to back.

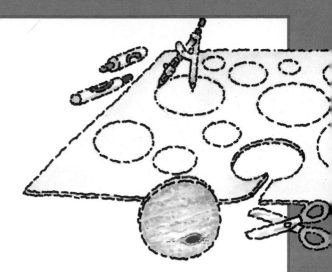

5. Color both sides of your sun and planets. Use the photographs in this book to guide you.

6. Use the large paper plate for Saturn's ring. Color just the outer edge of the plate, as shown at the right. Cut a 3-3/4-in. long slit in the middle of the plate, slip the Saturn model through the slit, and tape it in place.

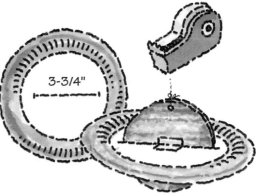

3-3/4"

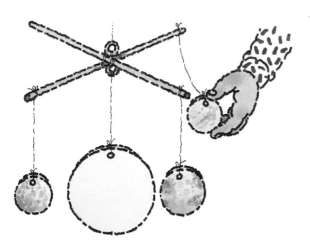

7. Punch a hole near the top of your sun and each planet. Tie your sun and planets to the mobile as shown at the left. Mercury, the planet closest to the sun, should hang from the shortest section of rod, Venus from the next shortest section, and so on. Uranus and Pluto should hang from the longest section of rod. Look at the picture of the finished mobile on page 19 for help.

How Planets Push and Pull

When people hear my name—Sir Isaac Newton—they often think *apple* and *gravity*. This has been my image for more than 300 years. So I've decided it's time for a change. From now on, when people hear Sir Isaac Newton, they are going to think *motion in space*.

Let me begin by setting the record straight. I did not—I repeat—did not

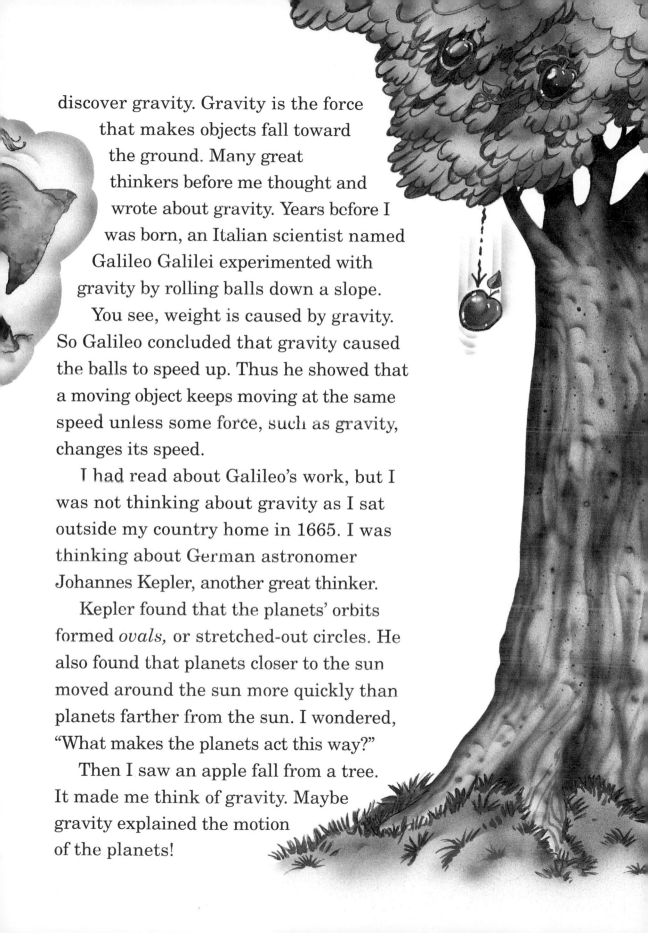

discover gravity. Gravity is the force that makes objects fall toward the ground. Many great thinkers before me thought and wrote about gravity. Years before I was born, an Italian scientist named Galileo Galilei experimented with gravity by rolling balls down a slope.

You see, weight is caused by gravity. So Galileo concluded that gravity caused the balls to speed up. Thus he showed that a moving object keeps moving at the same speed unless some force, such as gravity, changes its speed.

I had read about Galileo's work, but I was not thinking about gravity as I sat outside my country home in 1665. I was thinking about German astronomer Johannes Kepler, another great thinker.

Kepler found that the planets' orbits formed *ovals,* or stretched-out circles. He also found that planets closer to the sun moved around the sun more quickly than planets farther from the sun. I wondered, "What makes the planets act this way?"

Then I saw an apple fall from a tree. It made me think of gravity. Maybe gravity explained the motion of the planets!

I researched my idea about gravity and motion in space on and off for more than 20 years. Then in 1687, I published my laws of motion and gravity.

I figured out that a moving object will keep moving in a straight line unless some other force changes its speed or direction. That's my first law of motion. The force that keeps an object moving is called *momentum* (moh MEHN tuhm). My second law of motion states that the bigger and heavier an object is and the faster it is going, the more momentum it has.

These laws would explain the motion of a planet in empty space—the planet would

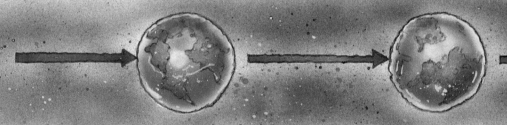

move along in a straight line. With nothing to stop it or push it in another direction, it would go forever. And a big planet would travel faster than a small planet.

You can see this for yourself if you roll a ball on a smooth floor. The ball will keep rolling in a straight line unless something gets in its way.

But things are different when you add a bigger object such as the sun. All objects have gravity that pulls on other objects. This pull changes their momentum. In our solar system, the sun's gravity pulls on Earth. As Earth starts falling toward the sun, it speeds up and gains momentum

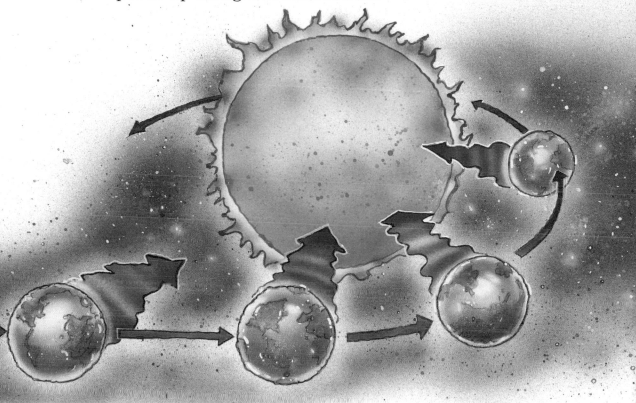

that pulls it away from the sun. This pulling toward and away from the sun happens over and over. It changes Earth's straight path into an oval orbit.

If you tie a ball to a string and hold the string while you roll the ball, it will move in the same way. The string's pull keeps the ball rolling in a circle around you.

Why does Earth orbit the sun instead of the sun orbiting Earth? Because, according

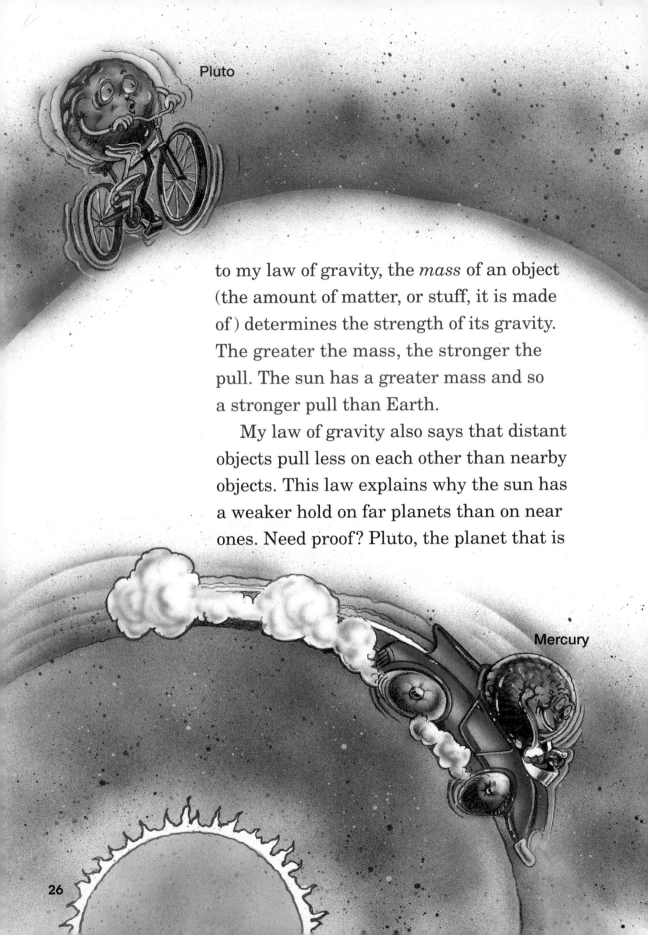

Pluto

to my law of gravity, the *mass* of an object
(the amount of matter, or stuff, it is made
of) determines the strength of its gravity.
The greater the mass, the stronger the
pull. The sun has a greater mass and so
a stronger pull than Earth.

My law of gravity also says that distant
objects pull less on each other than nearby
objects. This law explains why the sun has
a weaker hold on far planets than on near
ones. Need proof? Pluto, the planet that is

Mercury

farthest from the sun, orbits at a speed of 10,600 miles (17,000 kilometers) an hour. But Mercury, the nearest planet, moves 10 times faster.

I am delighted that scientists today use my laws to explain how the planets came to be. According to one explanation, a wheel of gas and dust once spun around the sun. Pieces of dust collided and became clumps. The gravity of large clumps attracted small clumps and eventually formed the planets. This process is called *accretion* (a KREE shun), and many scientists believe the planets really did begin this way.

Now what comes to your mind when you hear the name *Sir Isaac Newton?*

Snapshots from Space

Hi there. Cassini is the name, orbiting is my game. You see, I'm an *orbiter*. An orbiter is a spacecraft that circles a planet. I am also a robot because I operate with no people aboard. Instead, scientists on Earth guide me through space with computers and radio signals.

Watch for my name in the news in 1997. That is when I take off from Cape Canaveral, Florida. After reaching Saturn in 2004, my mission will be to orbit the planet and take pictures. I will send the pictures to computers on Earth in the same way that broadcast antennas send pictures to your television set.

I plan to drop a part called a *probe* into the cloud cover of Saturn's moon Titan. The probe will measure the temperature and thickness of those clouds. Meanwhile, special equipment will take pictures of Titan's surface.

My flight will be the latest in a long series of flights through the solar system. Over the past 30 years, orbiters and other kinds of robot spacecraft have collected information about all the planets, except Pluto. Why not Pluto? Because that small planet is too far away from Earth.

On these pages are just a few examples of snapshots taken by spacecraft.

Pictures of Mercury taken by the space probe Mariner 10 show a planet covered with craters and wrinkles. Scientists think the interior of the planet may have shrunk.

The Magellan (muh JEHL uhn) space probe mapped all kinds of landforms on Venus— plains, mountains, volcanoes, and

A photograph of Mercury's surface taken by Mariner 10

craters. Pictures even showed dunelike streaks of sand and dirt. These streaks were formed by the slow (between 1 and 2 miles, or 1.6 and 3.2 kilometers, per hour) but powerful winds on Venus. Galileo, on its way to orbit Jupiter, observed Venus as well as an asteroid, Earth, and the far side of the moon.

Unfortunately, not all robot spacecraft work as planned. The Mars Observer stopped sending signals after less than a year in space. Nobody knows why. The probe's goal was to find out more about the conditions on Mars. Scientists are not giving up hope of one day finding the Mars Observer.

The photograph of Venus below was taken by the Pioneer-Venus Orbiter. An image of Venus' surface, *below right,* was made with radar information produced by the Magellan probe.

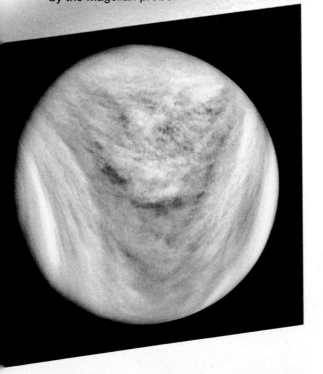

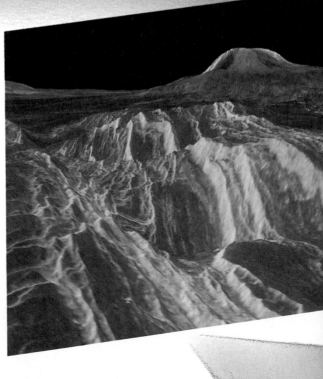

On the other hand, Voyager 1 and Voyager 2 have been sending signals to Earth since 1977. These spacecraft toured Jupiter, Saturn, Uranus, and Neptune. Then years later they left the solar system and entered outer space.

Aboard the Voyagers are recordings of heartbeats, whale songs, rock-and-roll music, and other sounds. If beings live in outer space, maybe they will find the recordings and somehow listen to them. Then perhaps they will send their own robot with greetings to planet Earth.

A close-up view of Neptune's surface taken by Voyager

Traveling the Solar System

Welcome to our solar system, tucked away in a scenic corner of the galaxy. To ensure a more safe and pleasant visit, heed the following warnings:

MERCURY: KEEP YOUR COOL

Half of Mercury faces the sun for 88 Earthdays in a row, while the other half faces away. While you are advised to be careful when you visit any place during its sunny time, this is especially true on Mercury. Temperatures here rise as high as 800 degrees Fahrenheit (430 degrees Celsius), which is hot enough to melt lead.

The dark side of Mercury is not exactly paradise, either. Temperatures there drop as low as -280 degrees Fahrenheit (-170 degrees Celsius). But if you bundle up in a specially insulated suit, you can survive the cold.

VENUS: BEWARE THE AIR

Venus ranks low on most lists of "must see" places. Why? First of all, its air is mostly carbon dioxide—a gas deadly to humans. Second, the atmosphere on Venus is heavier than that of any other planet. In fact it is 90 times heavier than Earth's atmosphere. That means that you could be crushed just by the weight of the air. And third, Venus' surface is hotter than any other planet—even Mercury. This is because the thick cloud cover around Venus traps in the heat.

MARS: BRING YOUR OWN WATER

Some scientists talk of humans someday living on Mars. But if you're planning on becoming a Mars pioneer, be warned: Bring your own water. Most of the water on Mars is trapped in icecaps at the planet's north and south poles.

Radiation is heat or light energy sent out from a source such as the sun, or in this case, Jupiter's extremely hot center. Some kinds of radiation cause radiation sickness, which is deadly.

CAUTION
RADIATION AREA
KEEP OUT

JUPITER: DANGER ZONE

Take our advice: Do not even think about visiting Jupiter. You may get burned if you do. Jupiter is surrounded by belts of radiation so strong they can kill a human in just a matter of hours.

SATURN: HOLD ON TO YOUR HAT

The strongest winds in the solar system blow around Saturn. They reach speeds of more than 1,000 miles (1,600 kilometers) per hour. This is about 8 times stronger than a fierce hurricane on Earth.

NEPTUNE: TIME DRAGS

Visiting Neptune? Do not plan on staying very long. One year on Neptune lasts 165 Earth years. You would need more luggage than you could carry.

URANUS: NO SWIMMING

Compared to the oceans on Uranus, Earth's oceans seem like shallow swimming holes. Their deepest parts reach down only 7 miles (11 kilometers). Uranus, on the other hand, is covered by an ocean 5,000 miles (8,045 kilometers) deep. But don't pack your swimming trunks just yet. At 4,000 degrees Fahrenheit (2,200 degrees Celsius), the water and ammonia that make up the ocean would boil you in an instant.

PLUTO: JET LAG WARNING

A fast jet from Earth would reach Pluto in 370 Earth years. So the flight could leave you drained. Still, a moonlight walk on Pluto might make your trip worth the trouble. Charon, Pluto's moon, is magnificently large. It measures more than one-half the size of Pluto.

Roll Over, Uranus

Astronomers consider Uranus a real oddball. All the other planets *rotate*, or spin, like tops. Their axes point almost straight up and down. But not Uranus. Instead, Uranus rotates sideways.

How in the world could astronomers more than 1-1/2 billion miles (2.4 billion kilometers) away know this? The moons around Uranus gave them a hint. They knew that most moons revolve around their planets in the same direction as the planets rotate. So when astronomers noticed that Uranus' moons were traveling up and down, they knew Uranus was special.

No one knows for sure why Uranus lies on its side. Many scientists believe that when the solar system was forming, huge chunks of matter zipped through and bombarded the planets. Perhaps a chunk

Axes (AK seez) are the imaginary poles around which the planets turn.

Axis

about the size of Earth knocked Uranus on its side, and there it has stayed.

The other planets tilt a little. On Earth, this tilt exposes the north and south poles to the sun for longer periods of time. This is why the poles have daylight for months at a time. But can you imagine nonstop daylight for years and years? You could if you lived on Uranus.

It takes Uranus 84 Earth years to orbit the sun. During this journey, its north pole gets most of the sunlight for 42 years, and its south pole stays mostly dark. For 21 of those 42 years, the planet's *equator,* or middle, soaks up rays, too. Next, the south pole moves to its place in the sun for 42 years, and the equator gets another turn in the sun for 21 of those years.

That is why scientists say there are two winters and two summers along the equator on Uranus. Actually, the seasons there do not differ much. The planet lies so far from the sun that little heat reaches it. So Uranus' atmosphere stays well below freezing during the summers and winters.

Unlike the poles of Uranus, the planet's equator has short periods of daylight and darkness, at least during its summers. Uranus spins completely around in 17 hours. So although a year on Uranus lasts 84 Earth years, its day is shorter than Earth's 24-hour day.

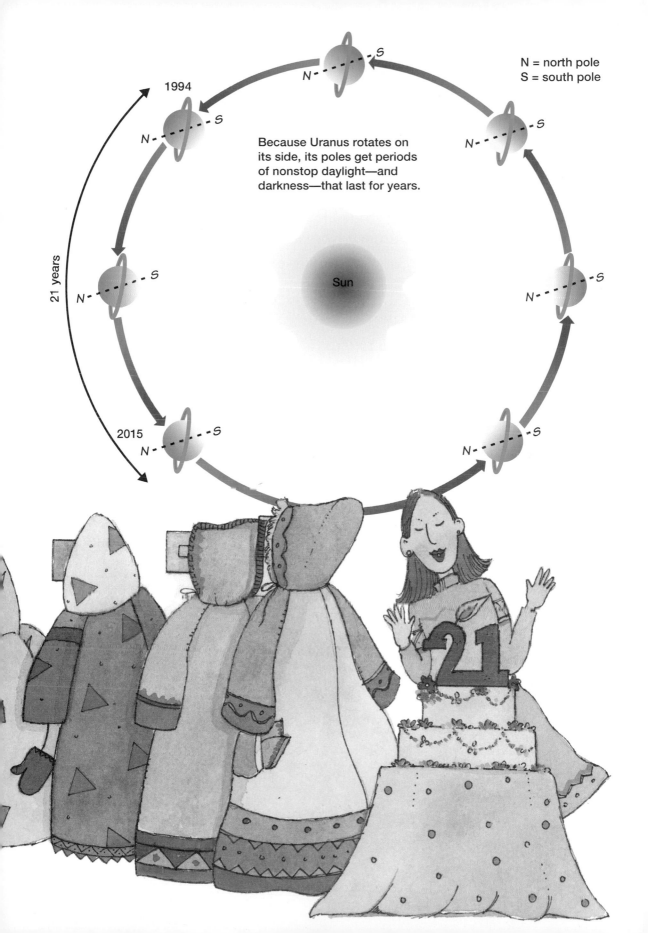

1994

21 years

2015

N = north pole
S = south pole

Because Uranus rotates on its side, its poles get periods of nonstop daylight—and darkness—that last for years.

Sun

Pluto: Ex-moon or Ex-comet?

Uranus is not the only planet with peculiarities. Pluto follows a strange orbit. The orbits of the other planets look almost like circles. But Pluto's orbit is a long, narrow oval. It looks like a rubber band stretched to its limit. The orbit is tilted, too. If you could look at the orbits of the two planets edge on, you would see that Pluto travels above Neptune's orbit at some times and below it at other times.

Pluto's orbit is strange in another way, too. It is not entirely outside Neptune's orbit. Where the two orbits overlap, Pluto's orbit is actually inside the orbit of Neptune.

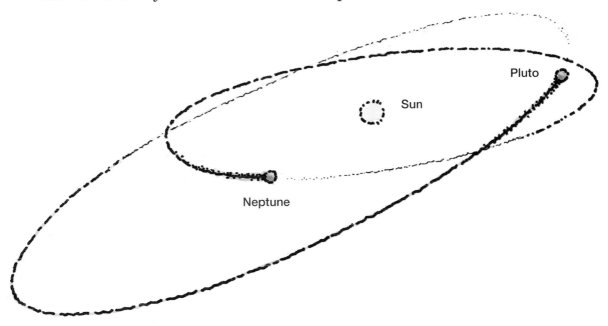

It takes Pluto 248 Earth years to orbit the sun. Most of that time, Pluto is farther away from the sun than any other planet. But since 1979, Pluto has been closer to the sun than Neptune because it is traveling inside Neptune's orbit. It will remain there until early 1999.

Some astronomers suggest that Pluto once was a moon of Neptune. After all, Pluto is only about one-half the size of Earth's moon. Perhaps, these astronomers say, another planet approached Neptune and swept Pluto into an orbit around the

The photograph above shows Pluto and its moon, Charon. The large painting is a view of what Charon might look like from Pluto's surface.

sun. At the same time, this planet broke off a piece of Pluto, and this piece became Pluto's moon, Charon.

Other astronomers point out that Pluto lies too far from Neptune ever to have been its moon. The distance between the two planets equals 18 times the distance between Earth and the sun. These astronomers also wonder where the planet is that put Pluto in orbit.

Still other astronomers think Pluto may have started out as a comet. Pluto's orbit does look similar to a comet's orbit. Perhaps a large object crashed into the comet and slowed it down. Then the sun's gravity grabbed it and sent it into orbit around the sun. These astronomers can even explain Pluto's moon. It could be the object that collided with the comet.

However, most astronomers believe that Pluto began just as the other planets did. Billions of years ago, it was a chunk of matter drifting amid the gas and dust that formed the solar system. Over time, Pluto attracted smaller bits of matter, and it developed into a planet. But Pluto never grew as large as the other planets, and it was able to capture only one small moon.

Science fiction or fact?

FICTION

"A tenth but as yet undiscovered planet causes wobbles in the orbits of Uranus and Neptune."

Fact: Astronomers have stopped looking for this unknown planet because the latest information from Voyager 2 shows that the wobbles were based on faulty observations.

A Star in Space

Clyde William Tombaugh

While Clyde Tombaugh was growing up in the Midwest, he worked on his parents' farm during the summers. In his free time, he built telescopes as a hobby.

Meanwhile, a wealthy businessman and a part-time astronomer named Percival Lowell was looking at the sky, too. He firmly believed in life on Mars. In 1894, Lowell built an

This is the telescope Clyde William Tombaugh used at the Flagstaff Observatory.

Clyde William Tombaugh

observatory in Flagstaff, Arizona, to watch the red planet.

Other mysteries in space also intrigued Lowell. One such mystery concerned "the Planet X." He thought a ninth planet was pulling Neptune and Uranus off their orbits. However, after a number of searches, Lowell was unable to find it.

In 1929, Tombaugh took a job at the Flagstaff Observatory. Astronomers at the observatory still searched for the unknown planet. They hired Tombaugh to take pictures of the sky over several nights. In his pictures, bright stars appeared as black dots. Tombaugh's job was to compare his pictures in a special machine called a *blink-comparator* (blingk kum PAIR uh tuhr) to check for changes.

On February 18, 1930, Tombaugh slipped pictures from January 23 and January 29 into the blink-comparator. He clicked a lever to view the first picture. He clicked again to view the second. Tombaugh noticed a dark dot that jumped when he changed the pictures. The dot moved too slowly to be an asteroid. He decided it must be the unknown planet he had been looking for.

Tombaugh reported his find to the heads of the observatory. They told Tombaugh to do more observations. The next evening he was back at his camera. Sure enough, the unknown planet reappeared.

The observatory director wanted to name the new planet in honor of Percival Lowell. He chose *Pluto* because the first two letters are Lowell's initials. Accidentally, the name also recalls young Tombaugh's role. The last two letters are the first two in *Tombaugh.*

Exploring Other Orbiting Bodies

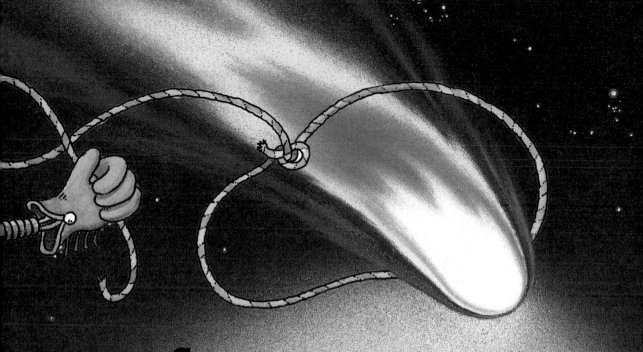

Still hooked on Saturn, Major Vox sensed his crew was uneasy. "While we're 'hanging around,' let's talk about other wonders of the solar system."

"Like those rocks flying around?" asked Little Rollo.

"Those are Saturn's moons," Major Vox said.

"Wow!" exclaimed Annabelle. "What's that bright thing over there? It has a tail."

"That's a comet," said Major Vox. "And it may be our ride out of here. Watch!" He pulled a lever, and SpacePod's Celestial Lasso spun out of a hatch in back. The comet's head zipped neatly through the loop, and the rope tightened around its tail. With a snap, the comet pulled SpacePod from the ring.

"Comets are cool," said Ben, as Major Vox reeled in the lasso.

"Well, no, Ben," said Major Vox. "They're actually hot, even though they're mostly made of ice."

Just then SpacePod started making strange noises. It sputtered and then went silent. Hard as he tried, Major Vox couldn't get it started again.

"Well, dip me in regolith—we've stalled," said Major Vox. "While I work on the engine, we'll talk more about comets, and about moons, meteors, and asteroids, too."

How the Moon Began

Howdy. My name is PAC, short for Pretty Awesome Computer. My name says it all. I am not just any computer. I'm a supercomputer!

Supercomputers like me help scientists figure out the answers to complicated problems. For example, now I'm helping scientists solve a riddle about space: How did the moon begin?

So far, scientists have four ideas to explain how the moon may have begun. My job is to make models of Earth and the moon. These models can show scientists

how things might have happened
billions of years ago. Now allow me
to explain the four ideas a bit further.

Fission (FIH shuhn) is the oldest
idea. The word *fission* means to "split"
or "divide." In the late 1800's, English
mathematician George Darwin thought
that the moon might have split off from
Earth. How could this happen? Billions
of years ago, Earth was made up chiefly
of melted rock. Darwin thought that the
effect of the sun's gravity combined with
the Earth's own spinning could have
broken free a chunk of this rock. But before
it could get too far, Earth's gravity caught
it. The chunk became Earth's moon.

The second idea, *coaccretion* (coh uh KREE shuhn), claims that the moon was made by the gathering together of dust and gas. Then gravity caused more and bigger clumps to gather in a large ball. Imagine squashing together little balls of clay to make a big ball. This is how some scientists believe both Earth and its moon were made.

Orbital capture (OR buh tuhl KAHP chuhr), the third idea, says that Earth's moon was formed far away from Earth, somewhere deep in the solar system. Then, at some point, it came wandering toward Earth. When it got near enough, Earth's gravity captured it.

Today, most scientists believe the fourth idea, called *giant impact* or *collision*. This idea says that billions of years ago, an

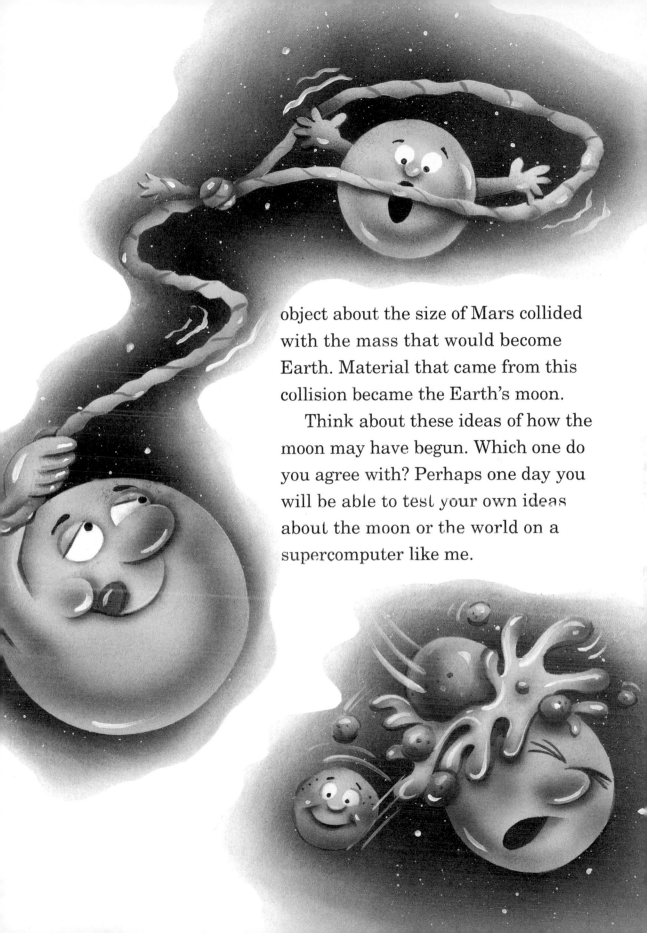

object about the size of Mars collided with the mass that would become Earth. Material that came from this collision became the Earth's moon.

Think about these ideas of how the moon may have begun. Which one do you agree with? Perhaps one day you will be able to test your own ideas about the moon or the world on a supercomputer like me.

The Man in the Moon Tells His Story

The Man in the Moon pulled out his notebook. "I've been around for billions of years, so it's time to tell my life story," he said. He began writing. Here is his story, in his own words:

Oh, how the years have changed me. When I first came to be, my inside and my outside were quite different than they are now. Billions of years ago, I was filled with a red-hot liquid called *lava*. Often, the lava would gush to my surface. This created large areas of dark rock. Earthlings call these areas *maria* (MAHR ee uh)—a Latin word meaning "seas"—because from their point of view, the maria look like water. But I never have had water. I am drier than the most parched desert on Earth.

Today, my inside has cooled. That is why many scientists say that I am "dead." Sadly, it is true—nothing seems to move inside me anymore, although no one knows for sure exactly what is at my core.

But my outside is a totally different story. You may wonder why my surface is so rough. It is not because I have a bad complexion. It is because I have almost no atmosphere to protect me from flying rocks called *meteoroids* (MEE tee uh roydz). Big or small, they smash right into me. They often leave behind large dents, or *craters,* and other markings. The impact of these space rocks also creates a dust that covers my entire body. Scientists call this layer of dust the *regolith* (REH guh lihth).

The regolith is many feet or meters deep. But if you ever visit me, do not worry

A ***meteoroid*** is a piece of rock that flies around in space. Most are the size of grains of sand or dust. But others can be much bigger. *Meteoroid* comes from a Greek word meaning "thing in the air."

The first astronauts who landed on the moon took pictures of their own footprints in the regolith.

that your spaceship will sink out of sight; the regolith is not like quicksand. Because I do not have an atmosphere like Earth's, the dust does not act the way it would on Earth. It is more like wet snow.

Because I have almost no atmosphere, wind or rain cannot change my surface. Craters, mountains, even an astronaut's footprints will stay exactly the same for years and years—unless, of course, a meteoroid hits them!

Another thing has changed over the years. You may not believe it, but I was once much closer to Earth than I am now. But we have drifted apart. I move about one inch (2.5 centimeters) farther from Earth every year. That may not seem like much. But after millions of years, it could

mean I'll be so far away that Earth's gravity will no longer keep me in orbit. I may just wander off into outer space, never to be seen in the solar system again.

And I go through changes every day, too—at least as far as Earthlings are concerned. They call these changes *phases*. Earthlings see sunlight move across my face as I orbit their planet.

When I am between Earth and the sun, my sunlit side is turned away from Earth. I am in the phase called the *new moon*. Although I am still in the sky, Earthlings cannot see me at all. The next day, a thin slice

NEW MOON

of light appears along my eastern edge, and I look like a crescent. Each day as I move around Earth, this bright slice grows bigger and bigger. When I am on the side of Earth opposite the sun, Earthlings can see all my sunlit side. This phase is called *full moon*. Then I begin to darken day by day until I am a new moon again.

But I'm not just a pretty face in the sky. I have a lot of pull around here. In fact, I can move Earth's oceans and seas.

Imagine Earth is a solid ball with large areas covered by a layer of water. My gravity pulls hardest on the water that is on the part of Earth closest to me. My gravity's pull causes the water to bulge slightly toward me. This is called *high tide*. High tide is when the water level at the seashore is at its highest.

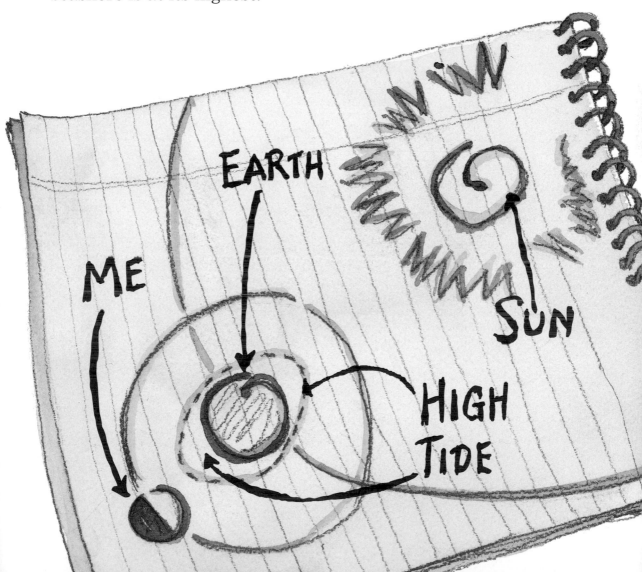

Science fiction or fact?

"The moon shines because it is smooth and reflects light like a mirror does."

Fact. While the moon may appear smooth, it is actually quite rugged, with hills, valleys, and mountains. And it does not reflect light like a mirror. The moon has a dark surface of dust and rock. It can't reflect much of the light that strikes it. If the moon were like a mirror, with a shiny surface, it would shine day and night almost as brightly as the sun.

There is also a high tide on the opposite side of Earth. Many scientists think that this is because solid Earth (land), being closer to me, is pulled more than the water. So the water is "left behind." This causes a second bulge, opposite the first. During Earth's daily rotation, these bulges move with me. In places where the water has no bulge, its level is lowest. This is *low tide*. Because Earth rotates under me, most shores have two high tides and two low tides each day.

Isn't that a good day's work for an old, gray man? Next time you see my face shining in the sky, give me a wave. If you look hard enough, you may see me give back a wink!

Study the Moon's Reflection

SPACE LAB

Things you need:
- pocket mirror
- curved mirror such as one an adult uses to apply makeup or to shave
- magnifying glass

1. On a night when you can see the moon clearly, set the curved mirror by a window so that you can see the reflection of the moon in the mirror.

2. Place the pocket mirror facing the curved mirror so that you can see the reflection of the moon in the flat mirror.

3. Look at the reflection of the moon in the pocket mirror through the magnifying glass. You will be able to see the moon close up, as if you were looking at it through a telescope.

4. Draw a picture of the moon as you see it. Be sure to include the dark and rough areas that you see.

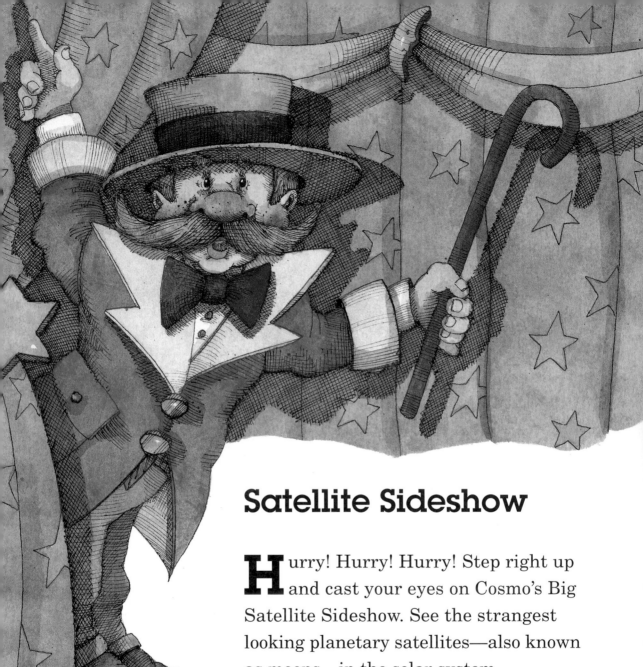

Satellite Sideshow

Hurry! Hurry! Hurry! Step right up and cast your eyes on Cosmo's Big Satellite Sideshow. See the strangest looking planetary satellites—also known as moons—in the solar system.

If it's weird, I've got it—moons that look like frozen pizzas or tumbling hamburgers. Moons that have been battered by meteoroids—and lived to tell the tale. All these and more. Step right this way. . . .

I'll bet you thought all moons were round and bright like ours. Just take a

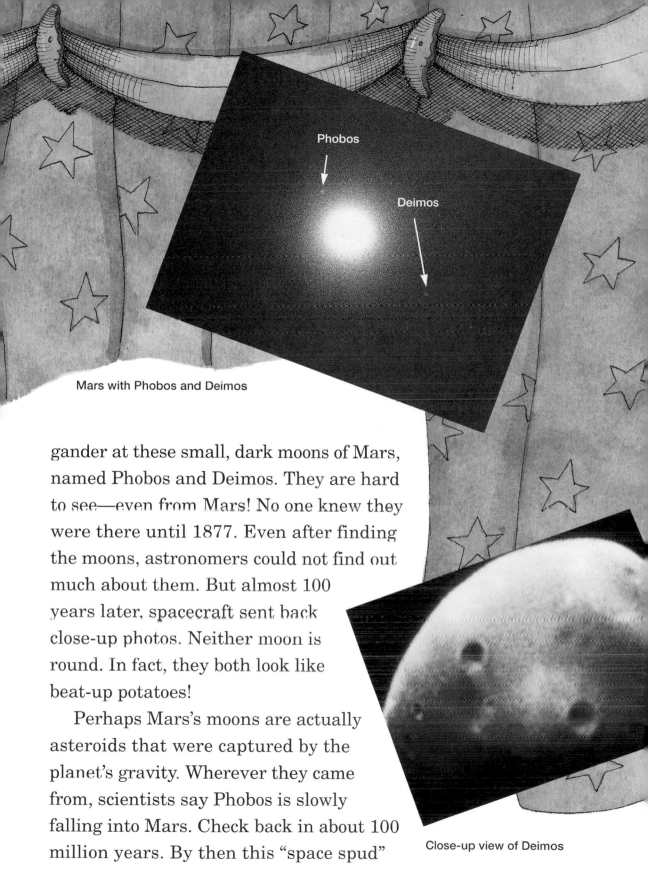

Phobos

Deimos

Mars with Phobos and Deimos

gander at these small, dark moons of Mars, named Phobos and Deimos. They are hard to see—even from Mars! No one knew they were there until 1877. Even after finding the moons, astronomers could not find out much about them. But almost 100 years later, spacecraft sent back close-up photos. Neither moon is round. In fact, they both look like beat-up potatoes!

Perhaps Mars's moons are actually asteroids that were captured by the planet's gravity. Wherever they came from, scientists say Phobos is slowly falling into Mars. Check back in about 100 million years. By then this "space spud"

Close-up view of Deimos

may have been turned into Martian French fries.

Now follow me this way to some of my oddest exhibits. They come from Jupiter and Saturn. Here is Io (EE oh), a moon of Jupiter. Its surface is orange, red, white, and black. Kind of looks like a giant frozen pizza—hold the anchovies, please! Photos from the Voyager 1 space probe show that Io is explosive. The probe's cameras took shots of erupting volcanoes on Io's surface. This is one frozen pizza that appears to be heating up.

Other sideshows may have a dog-faced man or a two-headed horse. Those can't compare to the two-faced moon! Out around the planet Saturn, the moon called Iapetus (ee AP uh tuhs) can't make up its mind. One side is bright; the other is dark. It is so dark, in fact, that a space probe could not get good pictures of it. Some scientists think one side is dark because it gets dirty when the moon travels through dark-colored space dust. Others think it may be the result of an ooze that seeps up from the moon's center. Yuck!

Do Not Miss IAPETUS, The Two-Faced Moon!

Saturn's
Moons—
Come
Watch the
Great
Chase!

But that's not all the weirdness around Saturn. Hyperion (hy PEER ee uhn) is a 220-mile (370-kilometer) long, hamburger-shaped moon that tumbles end over end in its orbit. And Saturn's moons Tethys (TEH thihs), Calypso (kuh LIHP soh), and Telesto (tuh LEHS toh) all share the same orbit. They chase each other around the ringed planet. But they never get closer to or farther from each other.

And of course there is Mimas (MY muhs). This moon of Saturn has been hit by so many meteoroids it is pitted like a

golfball. Scientists think it even may have broken apart as a result of being hit so often. Then gravity pulled the pieces back together. This may have happened several times. A moon that puts itself back together! Humpty Dumpty, take note!

That's the show for now, folks. In the years to come, new space probes will visit the planets. So look for more mind-bending additions to Cosmo's Big Satellite Sideshow. Hurry! Hurry! Hurry! Step right this way. . . .

MIMAS, The Amazing Puzzle Moon

The Sky is Falling!

My name is Chicken Little. Yes, that's right, the one who ran around yelling, "The sky is falling!" And of course, it wasn't. It was just a nut that hit my head—pretty embarrassing.

But I wasn't the only one to make that mistake. After I got bonked by that nut, I started thinking, "Could the sky ever fall?" I did some research. And guess what? I found out that a lot of people have been confused by things falling out of the sky.

Almost every culture on Earth has believed that comets and meteors were "messages from the gods." And the news has almost always been bad.

Now, of course, we know better. We have learned that comets are sort of like dirty snowballs. They are made mostly of ice, with dust and space "litter" mixed in. Scientists believe that most comets come from the far edge of the solar system. They think that a cloud of comets called the Oort Cloud exists there.

The force of gravity from a passing star may sometimes nudge a comet from the Oort Cloud into an orbit that will continue to pass through Earth's neighborhood. Scientists even can predict when certain comets will appear in our night sky.

But to the people of long ago, comets and meteors were unexpected visitors. People saw them as upsetting the normal operation of the heavens. Such a heavenly

Comet comes from the Greek word *kometes*, which means "long-haired." Why did Greeks call the comets long-haired? They may have thought the tail of a comet looked like hair streaming out of a star. One Greek legend tells of Electra, daughter of a Greek god, who tore her long hair when she saw the city of Troy destroyed. She was then placed among the stars as a comet.

change, they believed, meant that terrible things would happen.

Many ancient Romans believed that a comet meant the end of the current ruler's power. However, the famous Roman ruler Julius Caesar died a few months *before* a comet appeared. The comet then, the people explained, was Caesar's soul going to join the Roman gods.

You could say that other space objects do fall on us, though. Meteors enter the Earth's atmosphere every day. These chunks of rock or metal burn up as they enter Earth's atmosphere. They appear to us as streaks of light.

Sometimes Earth travels through an especially "dirty" area of space. Then many meteors can be seen in a certain part of the sky. When this happens, it is called a *meteor shower.* Once in a while, meteor showers are spectacular, with tens or even

Science fiction or fact?

"A shooting star is a star that 'shoots' through the sky."

Fact. A shooting star does "shoot through" the Earth's atmosphere. But it is not a star. A shooting star is actually a meteor.

hundreds of meteors appearing every minute. This kind of meteor shower is called *meteor storm*.

A meteor storm that occurred in 1833 created so much light it woke people out of bed. At times, there were so many meteors that those who saw the storm thought it looked like a snowstorm.

Sometimes, meteors hit Earth. When this happens, the meteor is known as a *meteorite*. Most meteorites arrive as dust that is too light for us to feel. But once in a while, a large meteorite survives the trip. Lucky for us, this does not happen very often. And because the ocean covers so much of Earth's surface, most meteorites land there. We usually do not even notice it when they hit. So, you see, I wasn't entirely wrong. A little bit of the sky does fall every now and then.

Comet Halley: Old Faithful of the Heavens

Edmund Halley discovered his famous comet in 1682. In this story, he tells how he predicted the comet's return.

I will never forget August of 1682. But I did not know until later how important its clear night skies would be to my work. I observed a new starlike object through my telescope. But unlike a star, this new object had a long, glittering tail.

I can't wait to hear what he says about us, Encke.

The comets talking in this story are real—Comet Donati was discovered in 1858, Comet Biela in 1772, and Comet Encke in 1786.

Hey, listen, Comet Donati. It's Halley talking about us—about comets.

"It's a comet, then," I told myself. I recorded the movement of the comet for a number of days in my notebook. The comet of 1682 shone very brightly. Even skywatchers without telescopes saw it. As the people of London, England, gazed up at the comet, some were frightened. They remembered the Great Comet of 1664. Soon after that earlier comet left the sky, a disease called the Black Death killed thousands of Londoners. Would this comet bring disease and death, too?

But I was too fascinated to be scared. I noted important facts about the comet's appearance: the time, the date, and the comet's position in relation to the stars.

For centuries, astronomers had studied the regular movements of the stars. We mapped them as if they were landmarks. I now used the stars to chart the path of the comet as August and September passed.

Stars were not the only objects in the sky with regular movements. Johannes Kepler showed that the planets traveled around the sun in *orbits,* or set paths, that were *elliptical*, or shaped like an oval. People used Kepler's findings to predict where the planets would be at different times. Unlike stars and planets, though, comets seemed to come from nowhere. And their journeys through the sky did not look like orbits.

I can't believe it! Halley isn't interested in us at all. But I, Comet Biela, am a special comet. I actually split apart during my 1846 trip around the sun. Two of me appeared on my next visit in 1852. Unluckily, my twin halves shattered before their expected return in 1865. Years later, pieces of them rained down as meteors when Earth passed near my orbit.

I observed that the comet of 1682 traveled around the sun in an elliptical orbit. The work of two scientist friends of mine supported this idea. Robert Hooke and I discussed the forces that hold the planets in orbit around the sun and asked ourselves how those forces worked. In 1687, Sir Isaac Newton published his great work about gravity. It explained how heavenly bodies behave when traveling near other heavenly bodies. I decided to find out what these ideas about gravity and motion could show about the paths of comets.

In 1695, I began to search the records of earlier astronomers for information on past comets. I compared their descriptions to the path of the comet I charted in my notebook in 1682.

Now, Biela is an interesting comet. And if you want the truth, Halley's comet is a bit plain. I, however, bowled them over in 1858. I had three gorgeous tails. I also stayed visible for more than nine months—an unusually long run for a comet.

You've always been a handsome one, Donati.

Seventy-six years? I beat that. I take just 3 years, 4 months to orbit the sun. I've made more than 50 trips past Earth since I was first sighted in 1786.

The comets of 1607 and 1531 looked familiar. They traveled in the opposite direction of most other comets. So did the comet I had observed in 1682! I knew that the three comets were the same one returning again and again.

The three appearances of the comet were about 75 or 76 years apart. I figured out that the comet of 1682 would appear again in 1758. No one had ever made this kind of prediction before.

Sadly, I did not live long enough to find out if my prediction was correct. But in 1758, other astronomers around the world watched for the comet's return. The first

Bravo, Encke.

Halley's Comet

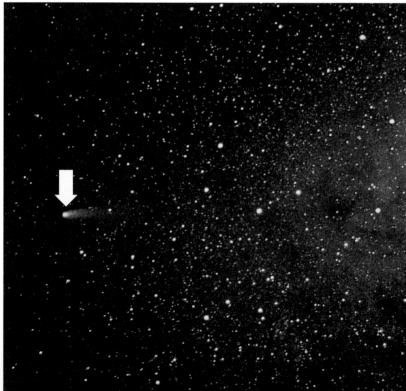

to see it was a German farmer whose hobby was astronomy. He spotted the comet on Christmas—December 25, 1758.

After the comet's appearance in 1758, people named it Halley's Comet. Today, astronomers also refer to it as Comet Halley. My comet returned in 1835, 1910, and 1986. You can expect my namesake again in 2061. Don't forget to keep your eyes on the skies.

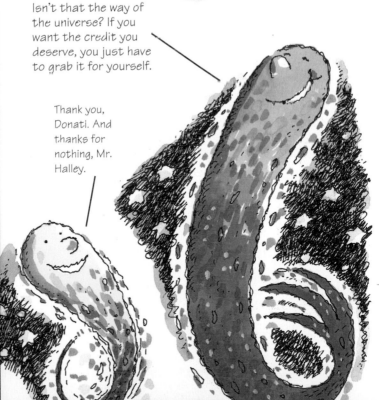

Isn't that the way of the universe? If you want the credit you deserve, you just have to grab it for yourself.

Thank you, Donati. And thanks for nothing, Mr. Halley.

A Star in Space

Maria Mitchell

Nantucket Island lies off the coast of Massachusetts. In the early 1800's, almost everyone on the island made their living either by sailing on whaling ships or supplying goods for the sailors. Nantucket's William Mitchell was a part-time astronomer. He used his knowledge of the stars to

Maria Mitchell

adjust the delicate timepieces, called *chronometers,* that captains used to figure out their ships' locations and course at sea. Whenever a ship came home from a long voyage, the captain would ask Mitchell to check the ship's chronometer to be sure it was correct.

Mitchell's daughter Maria helped him. She learned about the skies and how to operate a telescope. Maria also soaked up knowledge about astronomy from books. She worked at a library and spent her spare time reading. Eventually, she was able to adjust the captains' chronometers, even when her father was not home. Maria also kept careful records of the new stars she found in the sky. Sometimes her back ached, but each discovery made up for the long hours at the telescope.

On the night of October 1, 1847, Maria looked through the

telescope at a patch of sky she knew as well as her own street. In the middle of this patch, she saw an unfamiliar, fuzzy object. Maria did not trust her tired eyes, so she called her father.

William looked through the telescope. Then he checked the star chart. The chart showed nothing where the object was now.

"It must be a new comet!" he declared.

Maria knew that a comet was usually named for the person who saw it first and that the King of Denmark had promised a gold medal to a comet's discoverer. Later that evening, her father dashed off a note to the Harvard Observatory in Massachusetts. His note would establish when Maria made her sighting. But Maria dared not hope too much.

"Someone at an observatory must have seen it first," she thought.

The head of the Harvard Observatory assured Maria that they had not seen the comet before her. Over the weeks, reports trickled in about when astronomers in Europe had observed the comet. No one had spotted it before October 1.

Nevertheless, Maria waited more than a year before the

Maria Mitchell in front of her observatory in Lynn, Massachusetts

package from Denmark arrived. Her hands trembled as she unwrapped the medal. Maria saw Latin words engraved on one side of the medal. She translated them: "Not in vain do we watch the setting and rising of the stars." Below these words was the date of Maria's discovery. Around the edge of the medal was Maria's name. She was the first woman in the world to have a comet named for her.

Cleaning Up on Space Litter

On New Year's Day 1801, Giuseppe Piazzi, an Italian astronomer, noticed a star he had not seen before. As he observed it on the following nights, he could see that it was moving.

After watching that "star" for several nights, Piazzi decided that he had discovered either a new planet or a comet. When it returned the next winter on its predicted orbit, astronomers knew it orbited the sun like a planet. But since it looked like a star, astronomers called it an *asteroid,* a Greek word meaning "starlike." Piazzi named his asteroid Ceres (SEER eez) after the Roman goddess of the harvest.

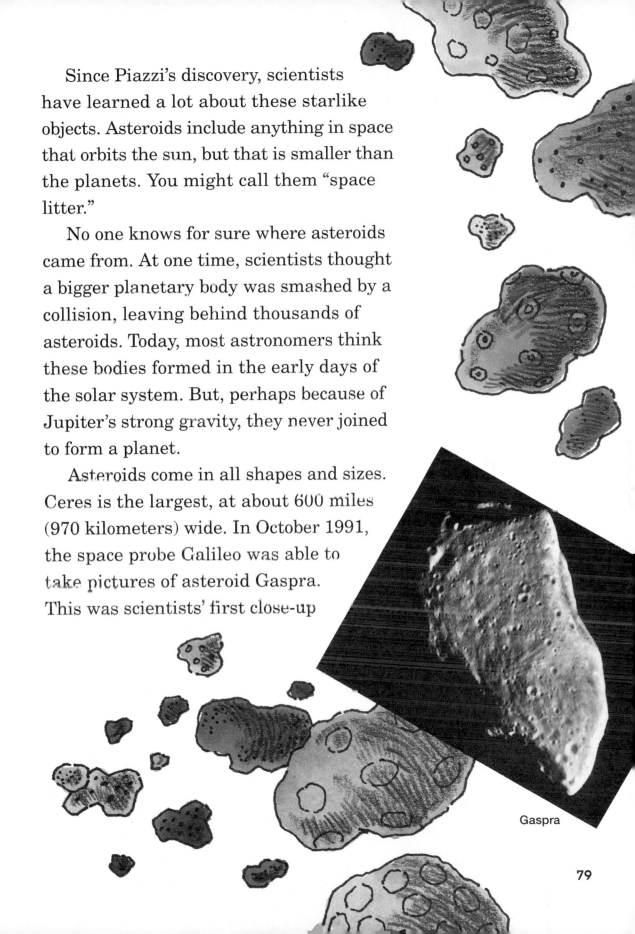

Since Piazzi's discovery, scientists have learned a lot about these starlike objects. Asteroids include anything in space that orbits the sun, but that is smaller than the planets. You might call them "space litter."

No one knows for sure where asteroids came from. At one time, scientists thought a bigger planetary body was smashed by a collision, leaving behind thousands of asteroids. Today, most astronomers think these bodies formed in the early days of the solar system. But, perhaps because of Jupiter's strong gravity, they never joined to form a planet.

Asteroids come in all shapes and sizes. Ceres is the largest, at about 600 miles (970 kilometers) wide. In October 1991, the space probe Galileo was able to take pictures of asteroid Gaspra. This was scientists' first close-up

Gaspra

view of an asteroid. And it looked just as they had imagined it would—like a lumpy boulder.

Most asteroids orbit the sun between the orbits of Mars and Jupiter. This area is called the "Asteroid Belt." But scientists have noticed that not all asteroids hang around here. Some asteroids' orbits slowly change, because Jupiter's strong gravity pulls them off course.

Once asteroids arrive in other areas of the solar system, they can be pushed and pulled by a planet's gravity. This is why they are able to crash into planets and moons. Some asteroids, in fact, have been spotted traveling in the neighborhood of

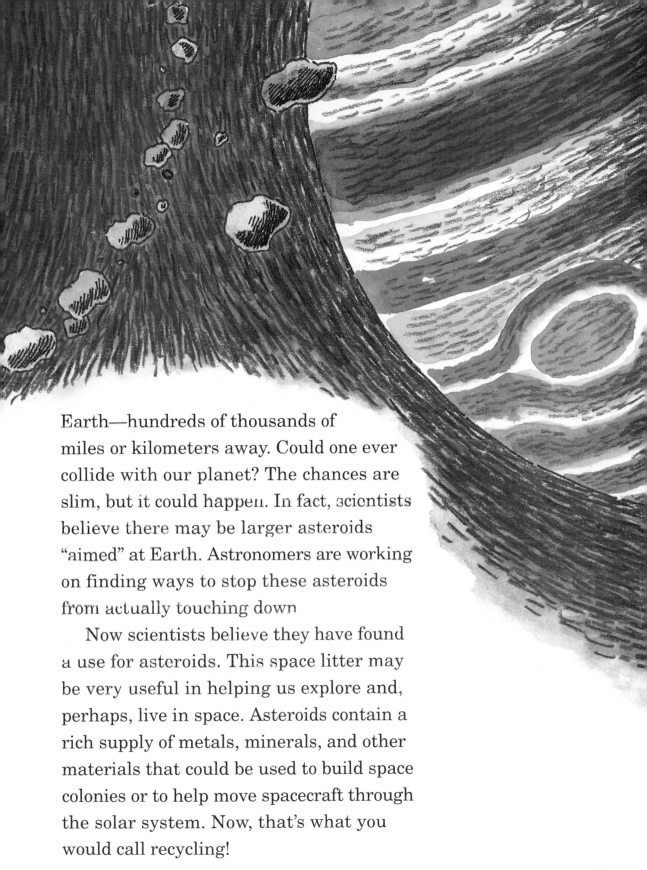

Earth—hundreds of thousands of
miles or kilometers away. Could one ever
collide with our planet? The chances are
slim, but it could happen. In fact, scientists
believe there may be larger asteroids
"aimed" at Earth. Astronomers are working
on finding ways to stop these asteroids
from actually touching down.

Now scientists believe they have found
a use for asteroids. This space litter may
be very useful in helping us explore and,
perhaps, live in space. Asteroids contain a
rich supply of metals, minerals, and other
materials that could be used to build space
colonies or to help move spacecraft through
the solar system. Now, that's what you
would call recycling!

Heavenly Pieces

Ready for a challenge? Here are some puzzles that are truly out of this world. First read the riddles for clues. Then figure out the answers to the riddles by putting together the pieces of the pictures. If you get stuck, the answers are on the bottom of this page.

1. When I'm new, I'm not at all bright,
   But my crescent's a beautiful sight.
   I shine when I'm full,
   And my gravity's pull
   Makes Earth's oceans rise to great height.

• •

2. I put on a long, shining tail
   When close to the hot sun I sail.
   I get dark and gray
   When I go far away,
   But I always return without fail.

• •

1) moo + n = moon; 2) comma – ma + jet – j = comet; 3) cast – c + er + oil – l + d = asteroid; 4) meat – at + tea – a + door – do = meteor; 5) meter – r + o + write – w = meteorite.

– c + er +  – L + D

3. I circle the sun beyond Mars.
   My name means "just like the stars."
   But really I'm rock,
   A chip off the old block.
   My "face" has "bruises" and "scars."

● ●

– at + – A + – do

4. I'm space stuff that just floats around,
   But I burn before I hit the ground.
   And when I appear
   In a sky dark and clear,
   With my streaks the heavens are crowned.

● ●

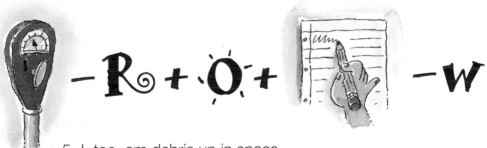

– R + O + – W

5. I, too, am debris up in space,
   But right toward a planet I race.
   With a deafening sound
   I crash to the ground
   And leave "stardust" all over the place.

Target Earth

In March 1989, an enormous asteroid passed within about 500,000 miles (800,000 kilometers) of Earth. This distance is a little more than twice the distance between Earth and the moon. If the asteroid had crashed into our planet, the impact would have been equal to the explosion of 10 atomic bombs! Destruction would have been widespread.

As Chicken Little discovered, Earth is often hit by objects from outer space. In fact, scientists think millions of meteors approach Earth's atmosphere every day. Yet almost all of these burn up when they enter the atmosphere.

Sometimes, however, meteors are too large to burn up completely. The leftover material crashes into Earth as meteorites. And these meteorites can be large.

There is a lot of evidence of meteorites crashing into Earth. What may be the largest meteorite crater in the world was found on the shore of Hudson Bay in Canada. It is believed to be 275 miles (443 kilometers) wide and much longer. Meteor Crater in Arizona is about 4,150 feet (1,265 meters) in diameter and 570 feet (174

Two views of Meteor Crater in Arizona

meters) deep. In central Argentina, along an area of land about 30 miles (50 kilometers) long, there are a number of oval craters. Scientists believe these craters are the work of a meteorite that crashed into Earth at an angle, then broke into pieces that skipped along the ground. To picture this, imagine a stone skipping across the surface of the water.

The largest meteorite ever found weighs about 66 tons (60 metric tons). It was found in what is now the African country of Namibia. In 1908, a meteoroid thought to weigh a few hundred tons exploded above an almost deserted area of Siberia. It was visible in daylight up to 466 miles (750

The largest meteorite ever found, *below,* was discovered in the African country of Namibia.

A meteoroid that exploded in Siberia in 1908 flattened miles of forests.

kilometers) away. People 50 miles (80 kilometers) away felt the impact of the explosion. The meteorite set a 20-mile (32-kilometer) area on fire and flattened entire forests.

Many scientists think that a massive comet or asteroid crashed into Earth about 65 million years ago. Some believe the changes in the world's climate that resulted is what killed the dinosaurs.

Now scientists believe they may have found the scene of the crime. It is an old crater nearly 185 miles (298 kilometers) wide in Mexico on the Yucatán Peninsula (yoo kuh TAHN puh NIHN suh luh). It was hard to recognize because it was so big, so old, and so far beneath the surface of the Earth. But its age matches the time that the scientists believe the comet hit.

Could a meteorite collision once again destroy life on Earth? Well, think about this: The solar system is filled with meteoroids. Many of them have irregular orbits that cross Earth's orbit, so it could happen. But scientists are working on ways to spot approaching meteoroids and destroy them, or steer them away, before they collide with Earth.

Create Your Own Craters

SPACE LAB

Things you need:
- baking pan or dish pan
- plastic trash bag
- newspapers
- 4-5 cupfuls of dry clay
- water
- several rocks, with a variety of shapes and sizes
- notebook
- pen or pencil
- ruler

1. Cover your work area with newspaper. Slip the trash bag over the pan to line it. In the pan, mix the clay with water. Make it soft enough to mold easily.

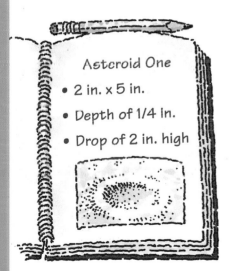

Astcroid One

- 2 in. x 5 in.
- Depth of 1/4 in.
- Drop of 2 in. high

2. The rocks are your "asteroids." Drop them into the box, one at a time, from different heights. To make some of them hit at different angles, tip the box.

3. Note each asteroid's size and shape and the height and angle from which you drop it. Also note how your "Earth" looks. Measure the depth and shape of each crater. Sketch your "Earth" with craters.

4. Now add enough water to make an "ocean" about 1/2 in. (1.3 cm) deep. Drop a few asteroids. Note what impact the asteroids have at sea.

Exploring the sun

Major Vox was worried. If they didn't power up soon, the spacecraft could be captured by a planet's gravity and become a moon. Suddenly, they heard the roar of a gusty wind, and sparkles swirled all around them.

"Hey, can I roll down the window?" asked Little Rollo.

"Better not, Little Rollo. Quick, Suki, press that red button," Major Vox ordered. "Sufferin' sunspots, the heavens have saved us again."

Suki pressed the button, and a shimmering space sail sprang from the bow of the ship. SpacePod bobbed peacefully along, like a boat on a blue lake. The crew breathed a sigh of relief.

"Where on Earth did that wind come from?" asked Annabelle.

"That wind did not come from Earth," answered Major Vox. "It came from our glorious sun."

"Wind from the sun?" asked Ben.

"You bet your quarks there's wind from the sun," said Major Vox. "And that's not all. . . ."

As Major Vox began his talk about the sun, Little Rollo froze in his seat, his mouth hanging open in fear. A huge bear hovered over the spacecraft, his sharp teeth flashing. "Please don't eat me!" Little Rollo cried, diving under his seat.

Solar Profile

Say hello to the sun. Want to know a little more about this fireball that provides light and warmth to our planet? Read on. . . .

Age: more than 4-1/2 billion years.

Width: about 865,000 miles (1,392,000 kilometers), equal to about 109 Earths lined up in a row.

Mass: about 330,000 times the mass of Earth.

Rotation time: about 27 days.

Occupation: center of the solar system.

Now do you want to get to know the sun even better? Take a closer look. . . .

Solar, which means "of the sun," comes from the word *Sol,* the early Romans' name for their sun god. We call the sun and the planets the *solar system* because the sun is at its center.

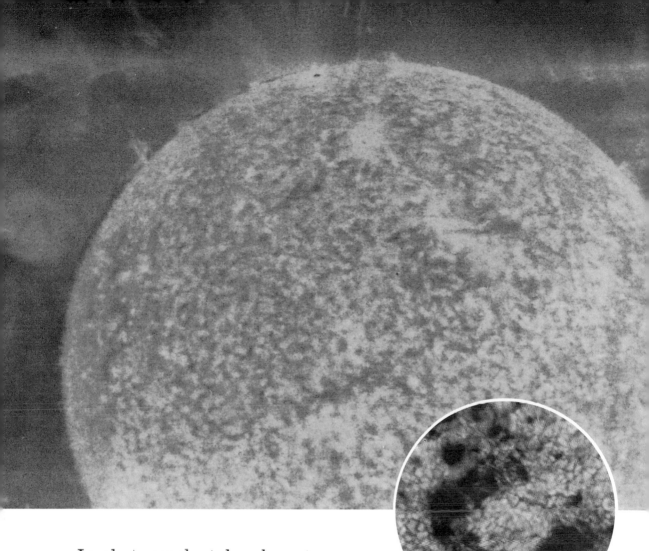

In photographs taken by astronomers with powerful telescopes and special equipment, the sun appears to be covered by millions of pebbly grains. These grains are called *granules* (GRAN yoolz). They look tiny, but a typical granule measures about 600 miles (965 kilometers) across! These grains do not live very long. They come and go like the bubbles on the surface of a pond. The difference is that bubbles on a pond are caused by air rising to the surface of the water. The sun's granules

Tremendous heat makes flaming gases erupt from the sun, *top,* and covers the surface with pobbly looking granules, *bottom.*

are caused by heat inside the sun rising to the surface.

Here inside the sun, you can see where all that heat comes from. Hydrogen atoms at the center of the sun smash together and form helium. These collisions release heat. The heat travels to the surface, where it spreads outward as warmth and light.

The temperature at the sun's center is about 27,000,000 degrees Fahrenheit (15,000,000 degrees Celsius). By the time

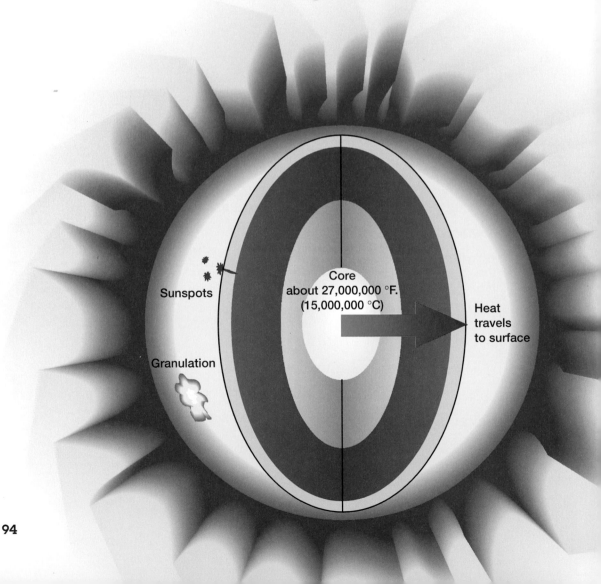

Sunspots

Granulation

Core
about 27,000,000 °F.
(15,000,000 °C)

Heat
travels
to surface

the gases from the center reach the surface, they have cooled to about 10,000 degrees Fahrenheit (5,500 degrees Celsius). Some parts of the sun's surface grow larger and cool even more, to about 7,000 degrees Fahrenheit (4,000 degrees Celsius). These cooler areas of the sun's surface appear dark to us. We call them *sunspots*.

Try to imagine how huge the sun is. Picture Earth at one edge of the sun and the moon circling Earth. The sun's width is equal to about 3-1/2 times the distance between Earth and the moon!

To us, the sun appears very large. But compared to other stars, the sun is not so big. Luckily, the sun is just the right size for Earth. Larger stars use up huge amounts of hydrogen and do not last billions of years as the sun has. A bigger star would have burned out before life could have developed on Earth. A smaller star would last much longer than the sun will. But a smaller star would not give enough heat to keep life on Earth going.

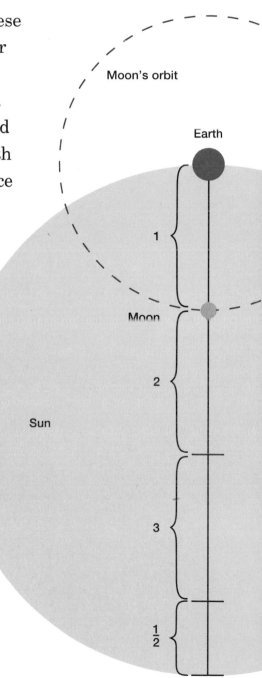

Where Were They When the Sun Went Out?

"Hsi! Ho! Where are you?" the emperor raged. "Come out, you sons of wild burrowing pigs!"

The emperor was furious with his court astronomers. They had failed to warn him that the sky dragons would return today. Now the dragons were eating up the sun. And Hsi and Ho were nowhere about.

Suddenly, panic overtook his anger. Bit by bit, the sky was growing dark. "The astronomers are no use to me now," the emperor growled. "I need my warriors."

The emperor called his archers and musicians to the courtyard.

"Shoot the dragons," the emperor commanded his archers. "Chase them away," he ordered his musicians.

A shower of arrows arched to the ground like dying wasps, and the clanging of drums and gongs filled the palace grounds. Finally, the sky shone bright as day again. The sun was saved!

The emperor sighed with relief and spoke to his captains. "When Hsi and Ho return, behead them at once." Then he quickly turned and entered his palace.

During a **_total solar eclipse,_** the moon covers the entire sun. Only the sun's ringlike corona remains in view.

An **_observatory_** is a place or building that has a large telescope or other equipment for observing the stars and other heavenly bodies.

In a total eclipse, light from the sun's corona may create a "diamond ring" effect.

The story you just read is based on one of the earliest mentions of a solar eclipse. It comes from a Chinese book that was written thousands of years ago, which collected legends, myths, and history.

A solar eclipse occurs when the moon moves between the sun and Earth. Astronomers in early China were among the earliest people to keep track of solar eclipses. But they did not learn to predict them until the A.D. 200's or 300's.

Many, many years later, on July 11, 1991, a great commotion again greeted a solar eclipse—this time, a total eclipse. A total solar eclipse cannot be seen over the whole world. Only those along the *umbra* (UHM bruh) see it. The umbra is a narrow

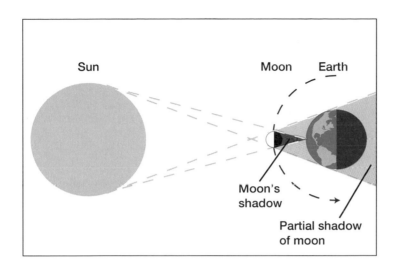

A solar eclipse happens when the moon passes in front of the sun and throws its shadow on the Earth.

path that is directly in line with the moon and the sun. It is where the shadow of an eclipse falls. That July day in 1991 was the first time Mauna Kea, a large observatory in Hawaii, would lie in the path of a total solar eclipse.

Tens of thousands of tourists arrived in Hawaii to watch the eclipse. Among them was a professor of astronomy from Massachusetts. He wanted to learn why the sun's *corona* (kuh ROH nuh) is 400 times hotter than the sun's surface. A corona is a sphere of dust and fiery gas that surrounds the sun and some other heavenly bodies. A total eclipse is the best

Science fiction or fact?

"Looking directly at the sun can damage your eyes."

Fact: Never look directly at the sun, even on cloudy days or during an eclipse. The sun's brightness can damage your eyes. And this damage can happen painlessly—so you may not know it's happening until it's too late.

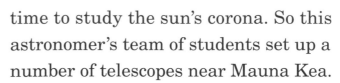

time to study the sun's corona. So this astronomer's team of students set up a number of telescopes near Mauna Kea.

Soon after dawn, they saw the moon begin to slide in front of the sun. Their excitement grew until, wouldn't you know it, clouds covered the sky. Much to their dismay, they missed the total eclipse.

Meanwhile, 50 scientists from France, the Netherlands, Great Britain, Canada, and the United States had a better view of the eclipse from inside the observatory. They filmed changes in the corona's brightness and measured changes in its

Scientists in a control room of an observatory measure and watch an eclipse of the sun, *above.* A photo taken with many exposures shows changes in the sun's appearance, *right.*

People use special glasses and viewers to watch a solar eclipse.

temperature. The head astronomer kept track of the experiments from a control room in the observatory.

Photographers near Mauna Kea busied themselves, too. One shot the cone-shaped shadow of the moon that was spread like a storm cloud across the sky. Another captured the blackened sun surrounded by a flock of fighter jets.

But a weather satellite miles off in space took the most dramatic picture of all. It recorded the long shadow that the moon cast across the globe. What might that early Chinese emperor make of such a picture? Perhaps he would see the tail of a dragon.

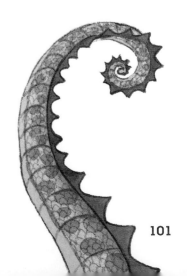

101

Sunspots and Flares

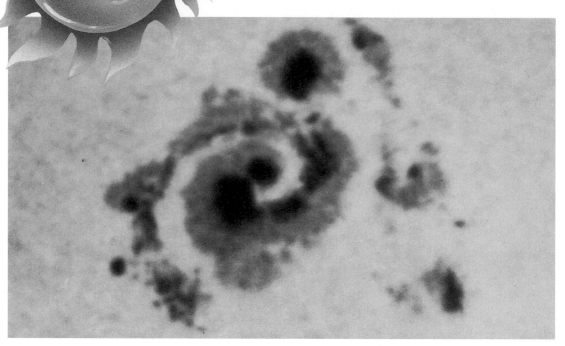

Pardon me. My name is Sol—I'm your sun. I'm here today because I must get something off my chest. My spots and flares have caused a lot of trouble for you people there on Earth.

A close-up shows a spiral-shaped group of sunspots spreading over the sun's surface.

You probably have heard about sunspots. To you they appear as dark areas on my surface. Each one is about as wide as Earth, and some are even wider.

The number of sunspots on my surface tends to rise and fall over 11-year periods, or *cycles.* I begin each cycle with just a few spots. Midway through the cycle, 100 spots or more may be seen from Earth. I reach

Very few sunspots may mean very cold weather. This old engraving shows a Frost Fair held in England on the frozen Thames River during the "Little Ice Age."

100 or more spots, and as the cycle continues, I have just a few again. Sometimes, though, I produce almost no spots for years and years at a time.

Scientists think that Earth warms up when my sunspot count is at its highest because the rest of me is brighter then. They also believe that the weather may cool when I have few or no sunspots, because I'm not as bright during those times. For instance, I had almost no sunspots between 1645 and 1715. During that time, Europe had a "Little Ice Age."

They called it that because they had such cold weather then. If my sunspots are to blame, I am truly sorry.

Scientists worry less about my spots than my flares. Flares occur especially often when I have many sunspots. They are huge explosions in areas around my sunspots. A large flare releases enough energy to supply a big city with electricity for about 200 million years.

Unfortunately, flares can do harm. Eight minutes after a flare explodes, powerful

Jets of flaming gas shoot from the sun's surface during a solar flare.

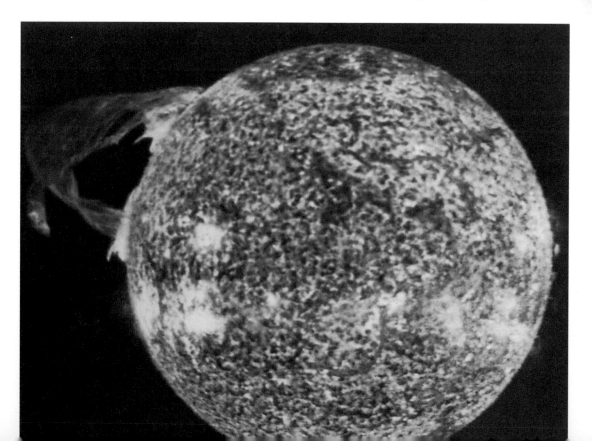

rays zap the Earth's atmosphere. These rays scramble radio waves.

About 24 minutes later, dangerous radioactive dust starts to pour down around Earth. Luckily, Earth's *magnetosphere* (mag NEE tuh sfeer) keeps most of the dust off your planet. The magnetosphere surrounds all of Earth except near the North and South poles. But this radioactive "rain" can cause a spacecraft to change its orbit and could hurt astronauts who are traveling outside the magnetosphere shield.

One or two days after a flare, magnetic waves wash over Earth like a storm. These magnetic "storms" can scramble signals to your television set. They also can interfere with electric power.

I feel ashamed just thinking about the trouble my flares cause. But they do produce at least one positive thing: They cause the shimmering lights that shine over the North and South poles to appear more spectacular than usual. After a flare in 1989, the northern lights covered so much sky that even people as far south as the Caribbean could see them!

Spot the Sunspots

Be sure to get permission from your parents before using their binoculars and tripod.

Warning! Do not look at the sun through the binoculars.

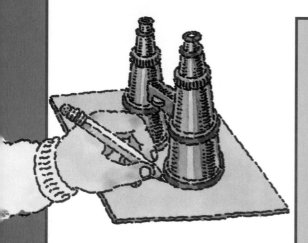

Things you need:
- binoculars
- tripod
- one 12-in. x 12-in. (31-cm x 31-cm) piece cardboard
- one 12-in. x 12-in. (31-cm x 31-cm) piece white posterboard
- paper
- scissors
- masking tape
- pencil
- tissue

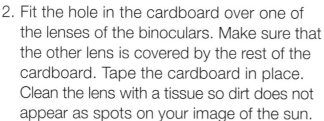

1. Place the binoculars on a piece of cardboard so they are centered on it. Trace a circle around one of the lenses. Cut out the circle.

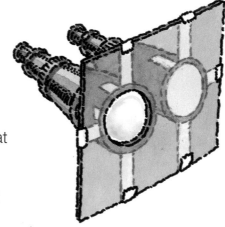

2. Fit the hole in the cardboard over one of the lenses of the binoculars. Make sure that the other lens is covered by the rest of the cardboard. Tape the cardboard in place. Clean the lens with a tissue so dirt does not appear as spots on your image of the sun.

3. Tape the binoculars to the tripod. Set up the tripod outside so that the end of the binoculars with the cardboard is tilted up, facing the sun. DO NOT LOOK AT THE SUN. Now look at the ground behind the binoculars. You should see a bright spot on the ground. If you do not see a spot, adjust the binoculars until you do.

4. Hold the white posterboard behind the binoculars so that the bright spot falls on it. Adjust the focus on the binoculars until the image on the posterboard is sharp.

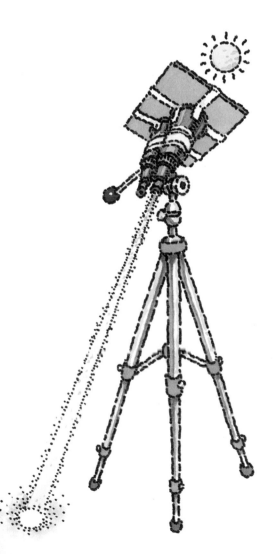

5. If you see dark spots (these are the sunspots), trace them on the posterboard.

6. Observe the sun for several days. Compare your drawings to see if the sunspots change.

Forecast: Solar Wind

Good morning, folks. This is your funny, sunny weatherperson with the cosmic forecast. Today's weather tip: Hold onto your hat. Solar wind will be blowing.

Solar wind is made up of tiny, electrically charged *particles* (PAHR tuh kuhlz), or bits of matter, that stream out of holes in the sun's corona. The wind that blows Earth's way may reach 2 million miles (3.2 million kilometers) per hour.

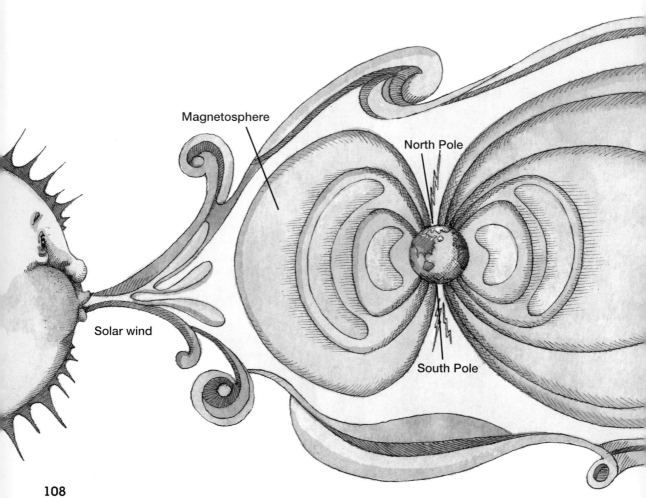

Magnetosphere

North Pole

Solar wind

South Pole

The aurora australis glows in the atmosphere above the South Pole.

Although solar wind is like an electric current, it won't shock you. Solar wind bounces off Earth's *magnetosphere*— a sort of magnetic envelope that surrounds the planet. Some tiny bits of matter become trapped in the magnetosphere and flow along its lines to the poles.

At the poles, the particles in the solar wind crash into other particles in the atmosphere. This makes them glow, like the gas inside a neon light. The glow fills the sky with shimmering lights. These lights are called *auroras* (uh ROHR uhz).

Expect solar wind in the days to come, too. It blows steadily from the sun to Earth, although the holes the wind comes from move around in the corona. The wind's speed changes, too. So stay tuned for the latest solar updates.

Old Man Sun

Many early cultures throughout the world worshiped the sun. No wonder! They could not live without it. They depended on it for light, warmth, and even food. The following tales tell about the sun gods of some long-ago peoples.

Re, the Egyptian sun god, had a hawk's head on a man's body. He made all living things from his tears. Each day, Re brought light to the world by sailing the sun across the sky in his boat.

The Japanese tell a story about the first solar eclipse. Amaterasu, the sun goddess, hid in a cave. The gods began singing, dancing, and laughing just outside the cave. Curious about the uproar, Amaterasu peered out and was surprised to see her own reflection in a mirror that the gods had made. As she paused, one of the gods took her hand and pulled her outside. The eclipse was over.

Lugh, the Irish sun god, was a warrior. His weapons were a rainbow, the Milky Way, and a living spear. With no help from Lugh, the fiery spear flew at the enemy.

Old Man Sun lived among the San, wanderers in Africa's Kalahari Desert. Light shone from his armpits whenever he raised his arms. The San children lifted the old man while he slept and threw him into the sky where his light could shine on everyone.

The sun god of the Zuni, a Native American people, sent his sons to Earth's people, who lived underground. The sons led the people on a difficult journey to the top of Earth. When they arrived, even the light of the morning star hurt their eyes. When the sun rose, they cried out in pain. But soon they could look around and see the many beautiful things in their new world.

113

A Star in Space

Copernicus

Long ago the Greek astronomer Ptolemy (TAHL uh mee) wrote that the stars, sun, planets, and moon all moved around Earth in perfect circles.

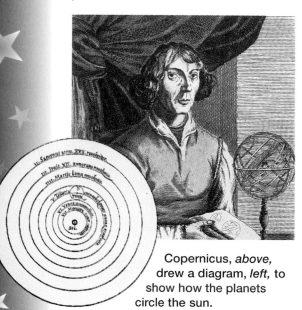

Copernicus, *above,* drew a diagram, *left,* to show how the planets circle the sun.

In the late 1400's, Nicolaus Copernicus (nihk uh LAY uhs koh PUR nuh kuhs) a Polish student, began reading astronomy books. He began to think the universe must be simpler than Ptolemy had described.

The stars must be very far away, Copernicus thought. So they would have to travel fast to circle the sky each day. Perhaps Earth turns each day instead.

The sun seems to rise and set, he continued, but if Earth spins around, it probably turns toward and away from the sun. So the sun need not move at all.

If Earth spins, Copernicus thought further, it may move about as well. Perhaps Earth circles the sun. That would explain why stars seem to be in different places at different times of the year. If Earth circles the sun, he concluded, perhaps all the planets circle the sun.

For many years, Copernicus did not share his ideas with many people. Since there were no telescopes yet, he could not prove them. But with friends' help, Copernicus' ideas finally became a book. At first, people refused to accept this new "solar system." But today, Copernicus, not Ptolemy, gets credit for starting astronomers on the road to discovering the way the universe really moves.

Your Place in the Sun

You deserve a place in the sun. To get there, ask someone to join you in playing the game on the following pages.

Use buttons as your markers. Place them on "HOME." Toss a penny to see who goes first. If the penny lands heads up, the player who tossed the penny goes first. If the penny lands tails up, the other player goes first.

Use a penny to determine how many spaces to move. If the penny lands heads up, go ahead one space. If it lands tails up, go ahead two spaces. Follow the directions in the space where you land. If there are no directions, stay put and toss the penny at your next turn. The winner is the first player to reach the last space—"YOUR PLACE IN THE SUN."

Your body uses sunlight to make vitamin D for strong bones. Run ahead one space, then take another turn.

ICE CREAM STAND

You get lost at sea. Find east by facing the rising sun. Then take another turn.

ART GALLERY

Cabbages on your Alaskan farm grow huge in the midnight sun. Go back HOME to make coleslaw.

Take a short cut through Sunshine Alley

Move ahead to the art gallery to see Van Gogh's painting called *Sunflowers*.

THE NURSERY

HOME

Direct sun helps your house plants double in size. Buy bigger pots at the nursery. Move ahead two spaces to the nursery.

YOUR PLACE IN THE SUN

Gazing at Stars

"**I**s there anything more you'd like to know about the sun?" asked Major Vox. Then he noticed Little Rollo shaking under his seat.

"What is it, my boy?" he asked. "See a ghost?"

A shaky, freckled hand appeared from under the cushion and pointed outside the spacecraft. The kids looked out the window.

"A bear!" they screamed.

Major Vox chuckled. "Yes, that's a bear, all right, but it won't hurt you. It's not a real bear. It's a constellation."

"A *constel* what??" asked Annabelle.

"A *kahn stuh LAY shun.* A group of stars that make a picture," answered Major Vox.

"Pictures from stars," said Little Rollo, dusting himself off and trying to look brave again. "Neat."

"I thought stars were just twinkling spots in the sky," said Ben.

Major Vox decided it was time to talk about stars. As he began, he failed to notice that SpacePod was headed straight for a dark point in space. With a loud squeal, SpacePod stretched to ten, then a hundred, then a thousand times its normal length. When the ship snapped back, Major Vox knew they had entered a black hole.

The Constellation Zoo

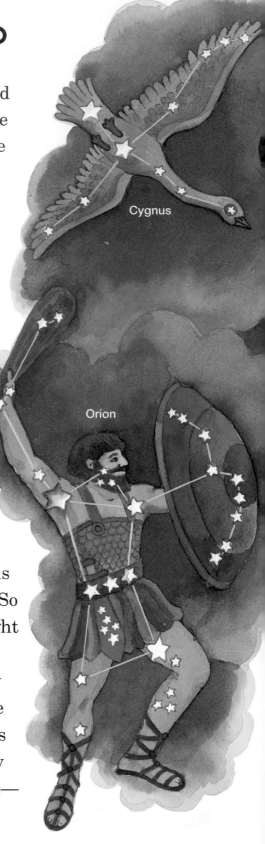

Cygnus

Orion

You've heard of "Lions and tigers and bears! Oh my!" right? Well, allow me to change that to, "Oh my stars!" because I am a constellation. *Constellations* are groups of stars that make pictures. My name is Orion (aw RY uhn).

Long ago, people looked up into the sky and noticed that certain groups of stars reminded them of an animal or a character from stories known as *myths*. Over the years, people named many constellations in the sky.

Aside from my job as a constellation, I am also a hunter. That is how I know that the night sky holds a zooful of birds, fish, animals, insects—and even dragons!

Some constellations are visible only during certain seasons of the year. This is because Earth revolves around the sun. So the part of the sky that you can see at night from a certain place slowly changes.

Take me, for example. You can easily spot me high in the southern part of the sky from December to April. Three stars in a row make up my belt. And two very bright stars—one red and one blue-white—mark my shoulder and my leg.

Pisces

Taurus

Cancer

Canis Major

Just to the east of me in the sky, you can find my two hunting friends, Big Dog and Little Dog. I call them Canis Major and Canis Minor. Sirius (SEER ee uhs), the brightest star in the entire night sky, is part of Canis Major.

What other animals can you find in the sky? Flying overhead on warm summer

Canis is the Latin word for "dog."

121

Ursa is the Latin word for "bear."

nights are two mighty birds, the eagle Aquila (AK wuh luh) and the swan Cygnus (SIHG nuhs). Cygnus is also known as the Northern Cross. It is easy to see Cygnus with its two outstretched wings.

We can't forget the two bears, Big Bear and Little Bear, also known as Ursa Major and Ursa Minor. Inside these bear constellations are the Big Dipper and the Little Dipper.

Snaking around the bears is a slinky constellation called Draco the dragon. You can see this creepy constellation almost all year around in the northern sky.

Science fiction or fact?
"A star twinkles because its light flickers on and off."

FICTION

Fact. Scientists are quite "Sirius" when they tell you that most stars do not blink off and on. Stars twinkle because moving air and dust in Earth's atmosphere bend and shift the star's light.

Then there's Taurus the bull. It forms a flying "V" in the sky. During late fall and winter, Taurus rises in the east about an hour before I do. Taurus contains the Hyades (HY uh deez), a cluster of stars you can see with your naked eye. If you look at it with binoculars, it is truly a spectacular sight.

The next time you look up at the night sky, see if you can find me and my animal friends. But as at any zoo, remember: Please don't feed the animals!

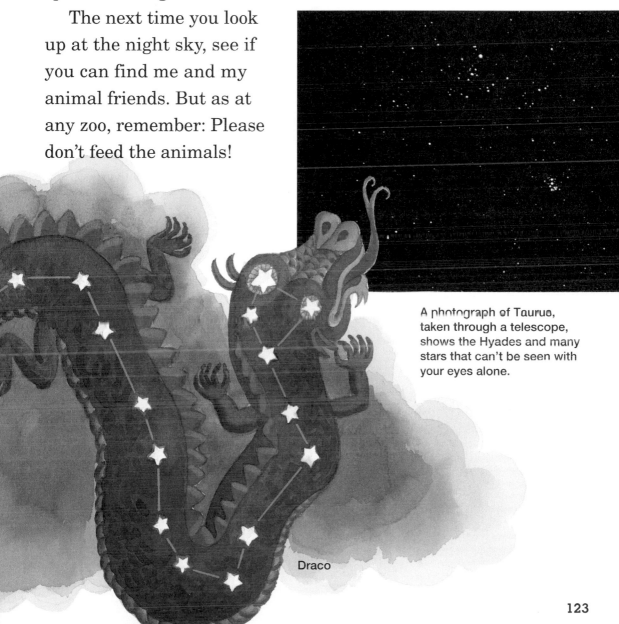

A photograph of Taurus, taken through a telescope, shows the Hyades and many stars that can't be seen with your eyes alone.

Draco

Things you need:

- oatmeal container with a plastic lid
- scissors
- pencil
- tracing paper
- black construction paper
- different size paper punches
- flashlight

1. Cut out the bottom of the oatmeal box and the center of the lid.

2. Using the tracing paper, trace the dots in the constellation on this page.

The Lion

3. Trace the outside of the box lid on the construction paper. Cut out the circle. Trim it just inside the line, so that it fits inside the lid.

4. Place the tracing of the constellation over the construction paper circle. Use the large, medium, and small punches to make holes for stars of different sizes. Or punch the holes with a pencil, making the ones for big stars larger.

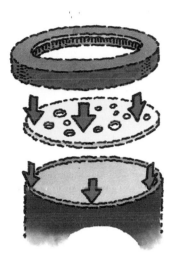

5. Fit the construction paper circle inside the lid. Place the lid on the box.

6. Go into a totally dark room. Put the flashlight into the box from the bottom, and turn it on. Look up. You should see the constellation on the ceiling.

7. Find constellations in other books and trace them. Then make more construction paper circles, and punch the constellations into them.

With your planetarium, you can stargaze during the day and on rainy nights. But on clear nights, go out and look at the real thing. The constellations will seem like old friends whom you recognize at a glance.

A Trip Through the Galaxies

This is the log of the starship Galactic Explorer. Our mission: to investigate and report on the Milky Way galaxy and other nearby star systems. What follows is a report on the highlights of our mission thus far.

Star Date: 2455.1

This is the first day of our mission. We're exploring our own spiral galaxy, the Milky Way. It has a bright central core made up of old stars. Around the core is a halo of ball-like star clusters. Outside it are several spiral "arms" like a pinwheel. A little more than halfway out on one of these arms lies the sun.

A ***galaxy*** is what scientists call any large system of stars, gas, and dust held together by gravity.

This painting of the Milky Way viewed from above shows its spiral shape.

Star Date 2455.8

It is a long trip across the Milky Way. Like our spaceship, the galaxy also moves. Just as Earth revolves around the sun, the sun and all the other stars revolve around the galaxy's core. We have calculated the sun's speed at about 560,000 miles (900,000 kilometers) an hour. But the Milky Way is so huge it takes about 250 million years for the sun to make just one trip around the galaxy!

The Large Magellanic Cloud

Star Date 2456.2

We have made our way to an irregular galaxy. This galaxy is called the Large Magellanic (maj uh LAN ihk) Cloud. *Irregular* means it doesn't have a true shape. The Large Magellanic Cloud and the Milky Way are both members of a small bunch of nearby galaxies called the Local Group.

Star Date 2459.4

We have reached an *elliptical* (ih LIHP tuh kuhl) galaxy. An elliptical galaxy is shaped like an *oval,* or a flattened-out circle. None of these galaxies have "arms" as the spiral-shaped galaxies do.

There are more elliptical galaxies than spiral galaxies in the universe. But that doesn't mean they are easy for us to see. From Earth, their shapes appear very fuzzy.

Elliptical galaxies come in many sizes. Astronomers know of a few elliptical galaxies that are 100 times the size of our own Milky Way galaxy.

An elliptical galaxy has edges that look fuzzy, even through a telescope.

Astronomers think that there are *clusters,* or groups, of galaxies. And clusters group together into vast *superclusters,* which can be several hundred million light-years across.

Well, now it's time to rest up. With billions of galaxies in the universe, the crew of the Galactic Explorer certainly has its work cut out for it.

A *light-year* is a unit of length used by astronomers. One light-year is equal to the distance that light travels in one year, or about 5.88 trillion miles (9.46 trillion kilometers).

All in the Family: Cluster Stars

This photo of an open cluster, the Pleiades, shows many of the smaller stars. The larger stars can be seen without a telescope.

Did you know that the sun may be an only child? The closest nearby star is more than four light-years away. Most other stars have family members living close by. They are part of *clusters,* or groups, of stars.

Look at the Seven Sisters, for example. Perhaps you know them by their family name, the Pleiades (PLEE uh deez). They are seven visible stars, along with many others that can be seen through a telescope, which are grouped together in what

astronomers call an *open cluster*.
You can easily see them in the
fall and winter skies, near the
V-shape of Taurus the bull.

Open clusters are the most
common kind of star cluster.
There are more than a thousand
open clusters. Some contain
hundreds of young stars. And
they have a variety of shapes.

Sometimes, members of star
families "move away." Over
millions of years, the individual
stars spread apart. Eventually,
the cluster no longer exists.

Some astronomers think that
the sun may once have been part of an
open cluster that slowly drifted apart in
this way.

Globular clusters are a very different
type of star family. Unlike stars in open
clusters, stars in globular clusters are very
close to one another. Globular clusters are
made up of thousands or even a million
older stars packed closely together. Through
binoculars or with the naked eye on Earth,
you can see that globular clusters look like

A globular star cluster

faint, fuzzy balls. And while stars in open clusters move apart, globular-cluster stars stick together, often for hundreds of millions of years.

What would it be like to live on a planet inside a globular cluster? You probably would want to stock up on sunglasses. The sky would be filled with stars. Many of them would shine so bright that nighttime would never come. There would only be never-ending daytime.

Another kind of star family scientists have found is two or more stars that orbit each other. Two stars that orbit each other are called *binary* (BY nair ee) stars. In addition to binary stars, three, four, or even more stars can orbit one another. Many binary stars belong to larger groups that include other binary stars or single stars. Astronomers call these groups *multiple stars*.

In multiple-star systems, strange things can happen. For example, one star may pull matter from another star in a kind of cosmic tug of war. Or the forces of gravity and rotation may change the shape of a star. And unusual bulges and barbell shapes are both possible in multiple-star systems.

As for the Seven Sisters, if they could talk, do you think they'd say they were glad to be from a big family? And perhaps the sun is happy to be an only child. After all, it shines so bright all the time.

This picture shows how one star in a multiple-star group can pull matter from another star.

Of Giants and Dwarfs

Greetings. I am Baltar, a giant, and this is Narni, a dwarf. We live in Fairy Tale Land. Did you know that amazing giants and incredible dwarfs also live in outer space? It is true. They are not people or creatures, though. They are stars.

First, you should know that the sun, the most important star to you folks on Earth, is a medium-sized star. It is smaller than a giant but bigger than a dwarf. The sun is 865,000 miles (1,392,000 kilometers) wide. That is not very big compared to giants.

You see, the sky has giants, and then it has supergiants. Giants are about 10 to 100 times as large as the sun. And, as you may have guessed, supergiants are the largest stars. The largest supergiants are about a thousand times as large as the sun.

Giants and supergiants burn their fuel faster and hotter than smaller stars such as the sun. They burn so hot, in fact, that they can be blue or white in color. Rigel (RY juhl), a star in the constellation Orion, for example, is a blue supergiant.

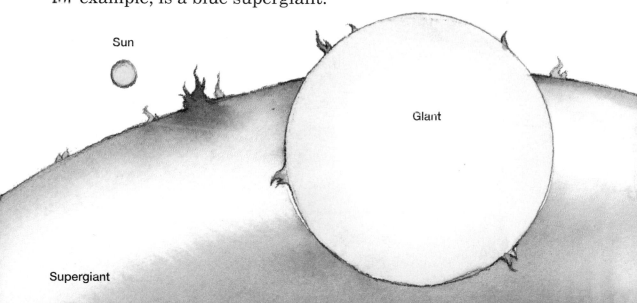

Sun

Giant

Supergiant

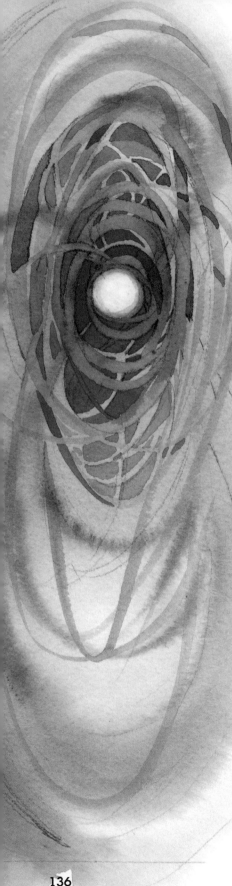

Because giants and supergiants burn fuel so fast, they do not last very long. Most last from only 10 million to 100 million years. That may seem like a long time to you, but for a star, that is no time at all. On the other hand, the little old sun has already lasted billions of years.

How does a giant come to be, you ask? Well, an older star eventually uses up the fuel that is deep inside it. It is similar to a furnace in a house that runs out of fuel. But in a star, when the fuel is gone, the furnace begins to collapse. Then the collapse itself begins to make energy. This new energy causes the outer surface of the star to grow larger. At the end of its life, a medium-sized star, like your sun, can easily become a giant.

But a giant does not have as much heat in the furnace as it did when it was a medium-sized star. So the giant is much cooler than it was before it grew. This causes it to be red. Such a star is called a *red giant.* Aldebaran (al DEHB uh ruhn), a star in the constellation Taurus, is a red giant. Betelgeuse (BEE tuhl jooz), a star in Orion, is a red supergiant 520 million miles (840 million kilometers) wide! That's almost 1,900 times as wide as the sun.

But that's enough about giants already. Let's hear some "small talk" from Narni the dwarf.

Thanks, Baltar. Let me begin by setting the record straight. We dwarfs may be mini, but we're tough heavyweights. As most stars grow older, they become cooler and cooler. Eventually, the old stars collapse. This happens because these stars no longer make enough energy to support their weight.

As a star collapses, the material that makes up the star becomes tightly packed. The star continues to collapse until it can't be packed any tighter. Then it stops. A *white dwarf* is born.

In its beginning, a white dwarf is about the size of Earth. But it contains as much material as the sun. So it is incredibly *dense.* Just a spoonful of matter from a white dwarf weighs tons!

Because a white dwarf is so small, it doesn't give off much light. From Earth, white dwarfs look very dim. Only astronomers using strong telescopes can see them.

White dwarf

Brown dwarf

Black dwarf

Over time, the white dwarf begins to lose energy. As it cools further, it becomes a *brown dwarf*. Finally, when the star is dead, it is called a *black dwarf*. It is like a blackened cinder in space.

Changing from a white dwarf to a black dwarf takes a long time. In fact, it takes so long that astronomers think our galaxy may not have any black dwarfs yet. It may not be old enough!

What about the sun? Will it ever die? The odds are pretty good that about

5 billion years from now the sun will become a red giant. Then it will become a white dwarf. And billions of years later, it will burn out and become a black dwarf. But that seems like forever from now.

For now, we want you to remember what you have learned here. And any time someone says that there are no giants and dwarfs, you can point to the night sky and say, "Want to bet?"

Special Report:

The Death of Stars

"**G**ood evening. This is Marcia Freeman for the Cosmic News Network. Welcome to our special report, 'The Death of Stars.' Tonight we will see a few of the unusual and spectacular ways in which stars come to an end.

"We begin with reporter Max Farley out in the Andromeda galaxy. Max, what do you have for us?"

Max: Marcia, we're here just in time to watch a blue giant star become a supernova. As you know, a *nova* is an exploding star. The star suddenly becomes larger and glows thousands of times brighter than normal. This brightness may last for a few days or even months. Then the star slowly returns to its normal glow. Astronomers think that a nova results from the explosion of material that gathers on the surface of a white dwarf.

The *supernova* we're witnessing here is another kind of exploding star. As its name says, it is even more powerful than a nova. A supernova may be thousands of times as bright as a regular nova.

A tremendous explosion in this supernova, more than 15,000 years ago, left a shell of glowing gas that is still visible today.

I think we're seeing something now. The star is getting brighter. What a sight! It's actually blowing its top layer completely away! A shell of glowing gas is forming from the layers. Now look! The shell is spreading outward from the supernova.

Marcia: What happens to the star itself?

Max: The remaining core of the star has now become quite heavy and compact. It's very likely that this supernova will become a *neutron star*. Neutron stars are the densest stars of all. But right now, Marcia, it is too early to tell just what will happen. So I'll send it back to you.

Marcia: Thanks, Max. Now for an up-close look at a neutron star, we go to Holly Rashad and a special guest.

Holly: Marcia, I'm here talking with a neutron star that many people say is the heavyweight champion of the universe. He says we can call him "Newt." Well, Newt, how did you achieve your great weight?

Newt: It wasn't easy, Holly. First I had to become a supernova. That took a lot of energy. Then I lost so much energy that I collapsed and had to pull myself back together. I became a tight, powerful ball of tiny bits of matter. Now I am only about 12 miles (20 kilometers) wide. But I contain a tremendous amount of matter.

Holly: Just how heavy are you, Newt?

Newt: A piece of me the size of a drop of water weighs about a billion tons. Compare that to some of the red giants in the neighborhood. Some are more than 10 million times as wide as I am, but we weigh about the same.

Holly: That is incredible, Newt. Your family must be very proud. Thanks for talking with us. And now let's go to Ozzie Vedder standing by in the Crab Nebula.

A *nebula* (NEHB yuh luh) is a cloud of gas or dust in space. The word *nebula* comes from the Latin word for "cloud."

BILLION TONS

Ozzie: Thanks, Holly. I'm looking at another neutron star, but one that has a cool beat. This neutron star is what's left of a star that went supernova and became visible to people on Earth in the year 1054. Gases from the explosion created what we now know as the *Crab Nebula.*

At the center of the nebula is a rapidly spinning neutron star. This star sends out energy in a steady *pulse,* or rhythm. So neutron stars like the one in the Crab Nebula are called *pulsars.* They can give off energy as X rays, radio waves, or even light. The energy is caused by the neutron star's strong magnetic field and its rapid spinning. But you'd have to have pretty fast feet to dance to this beat. As I speak, the Crab Nebula pulsar is blinking 30 times a second.

A pulsar's rhythm is so precise that scientists can tell which star it is just by "taking its pulse." That's why scientists marked pulsars on the maps they put on the Pioneer 10 and 11 space probes, which are flying beyond the solar system.

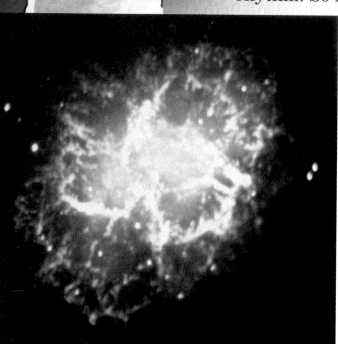

The Crab Nebula is what is left of a supernova that exploded more than 900 years ago. At the center of the Crab Nebula is a pulsar.

Beings in outer space—if there are any—who may find the map could use the "pulsar beacons" to figure out where the space probe came from.

Now back to you, Marcia.

Marcia: That is fascinating, Ozzie. To complete our look at what happens to stars when they die, we're going to Morrie Robbins for some terrific shots of a black hole.

Morrie: Uh, well, Marcia, the pictures we have are not too good. Actually, the truth is, we have no pictures at all. It turns out that no light can escape from a black hole. So there's nothing to show! I wish someone had told me. I guess I'll turn it back to you, Marcia.

Marcia: For more on this fascinating topic, stay tuned for our next feature, "Black Holes and White Holes," with your host Professor Everett Spacey. For Cosmic News Network, this is Marcia Freeman saying good night.

Marcia
Freeman

Black Holes and White Holes

Professor Spacey here. How do you like my wild hair? My wife says it comes from all the brain waves I give off. One of the problems of being a supergenius, I guess. But you don't need to be a genius to understand the wild universe of black holes and white holes.

When heavy stars (those that are more than eight times heavier than the sun) become supernovas, they leave behind a core. If these cores are bigger than neutron stars, their gravity is very strong—strong enough to reduce the core to a size smaller than a speck of dust.

The gravity from the core is so strong that nothing can get away from it. Everything is sucked into it—even light. And no light means total blackness. That is why these strange objects are called *black holes.*

No one can actually see black holes, of course. But we can see their effects. For example, we see stars that seem to wobble in their paths for no reason. We think that the tremendous gravity of a nearby black hole causes the wobble. That gravity also can strip material from a nearby star. And

A black hole is invisible because it pulls in light as well as matter. The picture behind Professor Spacey shows how one might look if it could be seen.

we can detect that, too. These effects have made scientists pretty certain that they see a star in the constellation Cygnus that has a black hole for a neighbor.

What would happen if a spaceship were to be sucked into a black hole? Of course, no one knows for sure. Some of my friends and I think it would be like entering a tunnel. We call the tunnel a *wormhole*. We also think that someone might be able to quickly travel great distances between galaxies or across the universe in a black hole. Then he or she would come out through a *white hole*, which is at the other end of the wormhole. On the other hand, it is also possible that the tremendous gravity inside a black hole would immediately tear anything that entered it to shreds.

Wild stuff, huh? Well, don't start packing for a trip through a wormhole just yet. These are still just ideas. But in trying to prove them, scientists are showing everyone what an incredible universe we live in.

A Star in Space

Stephen Hawking

How is it that we know so much about black holes? We have the British scientist Stephen Hawking to thank for much of that. He has helped everyone better understand black holes. He has shown that black holes do not last forever. According to his ideas, they slowly give off radiation and tiny bits of matter until they eventually explode and disappear.

Hawking also helped show that black holes can have only certain shapes and sizes. This helps scientists searching for real black holes to know where to look and whether they have found one or not.

Hawking also believes that black holes may actually generate energy by their effect on nearby space, even as they suck in everything around them. He says that some "black holes ain't so black." In fact, they may be white hot!

Hawking has been confined to a wheelchair for many years with a crippling disease called ALS, or Lou Gehrig's disease. Since 1985, he also has been unable to speak, so he has to use computers to communicate. Even so, Hawking continues to work on scientific problems, like black holes, that lie at the frontiers of human imagination.

Appearing on an episode of "Star Trek: The Next Generation," Stephen Hawking, *center,* meets famous scientists of the past, including Albert Einstein, *left.*

Touring the Universe

As every space traveler knows, falling into a black hole can mean serious trouble. But Major Vox didn't want to frighten his young companions.

"We're traveling along in a kind of tunnel called a 'wormhole,'" said Major Vox. "Not even I know much about these critters."

Then Suki piped up: "Major Vox, once I saw a movie where a ship escaped a black hole by traveling at the speed of light."

"I'm afraid that won't work," Major Vox said. "Not even light can escape from a black hole."

"What will we do?" Ben asked.

"We'll have to get to the end of this wormhole and see where in the starry heavens we'll end up," Major Vox answered.

Suddenly, with a great, loud THWOP, they burst through a white hole and out of the wormhole.

"Yayyyy!! We're out!!" the kids cried.

But then Major Vox's green face went pale. "Leapin' logarithms, my instruments are giving strange readings," he said to himself. "Oh no, we've gone too far. . . ." He turned to the kids. "We're on a tiny detour," he said cheerfully, pretending nothing was wrong. "It's 12:30 now. During lunch, I'll explain the speed of light and other neat things."

Early Skywatchers

Carmella and Raoul always look forward to visiting Aunt Snow Moon. Her work as an archaeoastronomer (ahr kee uh uh STRAHN uh muhr) takes her all over the Americas. She brings back wonderful stories the way other travelers bring back souvenirs.

"What did you see in Wyoming?" Carmella asked after kissing her aunt.

"The Big Horn Medicine Wheel, my child," Snow Moon answered.

"Tell us more," Raoul begged.

"It's a circle of stones with a large stone pile called a *cairn* (kairn) at the center. Rows of stones stretch out from the center to smaller cairns around the circle," Aunt Snow Moon replied.

"What's it for?" Raoul asked.

"To observe the stars," she answered. "Native Americans built the medicine wheel around 2,000 years ago. From each small cairn, they could watch a different bright star rise over the cairn in the center.

"Many groups of early Native Americans built observatories. They had no calendars as we have today. They would use the observatories to watch the sun and stars.

The stars told them when to plant crops or when to move to winter homes."

"Did the stars actually talk to them?" Raoul wanted to know.

"No, but the stars always appeared at the same place in a certain season," Snow Moon told him.

"What did the first Americans think the rest of space was like?" Carmella asked.

"Most groups thought that the place they lived was the center of the universe. To the Navajo, who

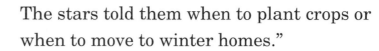

Big Horn Medicine Wheel, Wyoming

lived in a hot, dry desert, the rainbow was a god, and the sky was their father. Above the sky lay a land ruled by wind and thunder.

"The early Maya in what is now Central America believed their universe rested on the back of a crocodile in a vast sea. Four beings held up the heavens as if it were a great bowl. To Mayan eyes, the stars in the Seven Sisters constellation formed a rattlesnake's tail. And the dark shadows on the moon formed the image of a rabbit rather than a face.

"For the Inca of South America, the Milky Way flowed through the underworld and back to the sky. Inside this river of

Science fiction or fact?

"Columbus was the first person to think Earth was round."

Fact: Early Greek scientists such as Aristotle and Ptolemy wrote that the Earth was a sphere. Later, many people insisted this was impossible, for on the underside of a globe, people would walk upside down. But Christopher Columbus and other educated seafarers of his time read Ptolemy's work and believed his ideas.

In the Navajo world, *above*, the rainbow god arches above the Earth as Big Wind and Big Thunder watch over the sky beyond. A Mayan observatory, *left,* still stands in the ruins of Chichén Itzá in Mexico.

stars, the Inca saw a snake, a toad, a fox, two birds, and two llamas—a mother and her baby. The heavens must have seemed a lot like home to the Inca."

"You know, Auntie Snow Moon, you are really an astronaut. But you explore past universes instead of flying to the moon," Raoul said.

"That's exactly right, my dear," Snow Moon agreed with a proud smile.

155

Light-Years Away

A **wave** is a pulse of energy through the air or some other matter, such as water.

Meet the fastest traveler in the universe. My name is Lotta Light, and I zip around space at about 186,282 miles (299,792 kilometers) per second.

Long ago, most people thought light traveled at a speed too fast to measure. That didn't keep early scientists from trying, though. The first was the Italian scientist and inventor Galileo Galilei. He attempted to measure the time light from a lantern took to travel between hilltops. But in Galileo's time, there

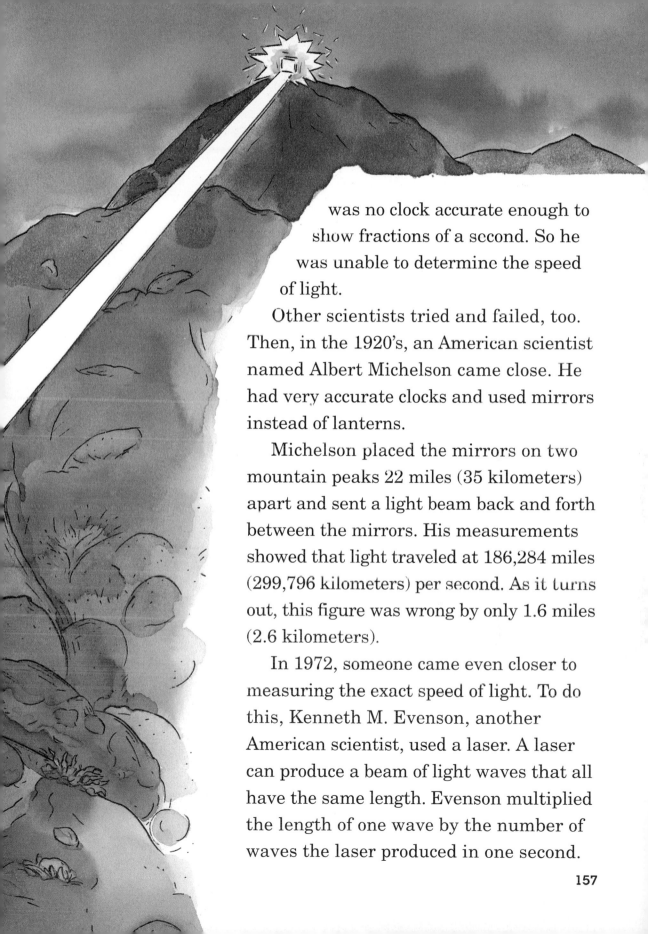

was no clock accurate enough to show fractions of a second. So he was unable to determine the speed of light.

Other scientists tried and failed, too. Then, in the 1920's, an American scientist named Albert Michelson came close. He had very accurate clocks and used mirrors instead of lanterns.

Michelson placed the mirrors on two mountain peaks 22 miles (35 kilometers) apart and sent a light beam back and forth between the mirrors. His measurements showed that light traveled at 186,284 miles (299,796 kilometers) per second. As it turns out, this figure was wrong by only 1.6 miles (2.6 kilometers).

In 1972, someone came even closer to measuring the exact speed of light. To do this, Kenneth M. Evenson, another American scientist, used a laser. A laser can produce a beam of light waves that all have the same length. Evenson multiplied the length of one wave by the number of waves the laser produced in one second.

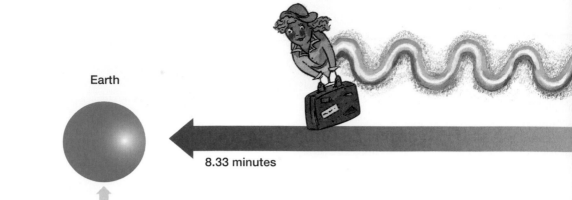

Earth

8.33 minutes

1.25 seconds

Moon

His answer was 186,282.3959 miles (299,792.4562 kilometers).

Today, astronomers use the speed of light to describe distances in space. For example, moonlight takes 1-1/3 seconds to reach Earth. So astronomers say that the moon is 1-1/3 light-seconds away. Sunlight reaches Earth in 8-1/3 minutes. So the sun is 8-1/3 light-minutes away.

A light-year is equal to the distance light travels in a year. This distance is about 6 trillion miles (9.5 trillion kilometers). That is equal to about 65 million times the distance between the sun and Earth.

Sirius, a "neighboring" star, lies about nine light-years away from Earth. So the light you see now left the star about nine years ago. That means when you look at Sirius, you're seeing it as it was when you were very little or perhaps even before you were born.

Sun

The distance across the Milky Way is about 100,000 light-years. And 100,000 years is how long I, Lotta Light, must travel to cross it.

If you will excuse me now, I have no time to waste. I am on my way to the stars.

This photo of the Milky Way was taken from a satellite. Light from the center traveled about 28,000 years before reaching the camera.

A Star in Space

Edwin Hubble

Edwin Hubble was hooked on astronomy by the time he was 12. But he had other interests, too. In high school and college, he boxed, played football, and was captain of the track team.

Hubble did very well in his studies, as well as in sports. He

Edwin Hubble sitting in the observer's cage inside the Hale telescope at Mount Palomar, California

won a *scholarship* (money) to attend college, and he wanted to become a lawyer. But he soon gave up law for his first love—astronomy.

In 1919, Hubble was working at the Mount Wilson Observatory in California. There he used a new 100-inch (254-centimeter) telescope to take pictures of certain nebulas. At the time, many astronomers thought that these nebulas were gas clouds in the Milky Way, and that the Milky Way was the only galaxy in the universe.

Hubble's pictures showed that the nebulas were made up of stars, not gas. Hubble figured out that the closest of these star groups lay about 2 million light-years away—far beyond the limits of the Milky Way. The most distant star groups lay hundreds of times farther. The nebulas, then, were galaxies. Suddenly the universe was much larger!

For years, astronomers have determined the direction a star moves by observing the star's *Doppler shift.* What's Doppler shift? Light waves get shorter and bunch together when they come toward you and stretch out as they move away. Short light waves are blue. So when stars move toward Earth, their bunched-together light waves appear blue. Stars moving toward us have *blue shifts.* Red light has a long wavelength. So when stars move away from Earth, their spread-out light waves appear red. These stars have *red shifts.*

Within the Milky Way, half the stars have blue shifts and the rest have red shifts. Most travel less than 50 miles (80 kilometers) per second. Many astronomers thought the newly discovered galaxies would fit the same pattern—as many approaching us as moving away and all traveling slowly through space.

To his surprise, Hubble found that all the faraway galaxies had red shifts. He also observed that the more distant a galaxy was, the faster it raced away from the Milky Way. After 10 years of observations and calculations, Hubble concluded that the whole universe was expanding, or growing larger.

Thanks to Hubble, astronomers discovered a changing universe. And because the universe was changing, the way scientists did astronomy had to change, too. Neither would ever be the same again.

How Did the Universe Begin?

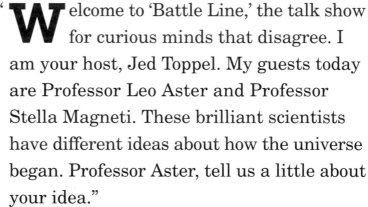

Elements are the simplest chemical substances. Elements can't be broken up into other chemical substances. Gold, oxygen, lead, and chlorine are all elements.

"**W**elcome to 'Battle Line,' the talk show for curious minds that disagree. I am your host, Jed Toppel. My guests today are Professor Leo Aster and Professor Stella Magneti. These brilliant scientists have different ideas about how the universe began. Professor Aster, tell us a little about your idea."

Aster: Well, Jed, I call it the "big bang." We know that the galaxies have been moving apart for billions of years. So they must have started out much closer together, right? In fact, my fellow scientists and I believe that all the matter in the universe once was packed into a single point much tinier than an ant. But this point probably weighed more than 10 billion trillion stars.

Toppel: That's a heavy ant.

Aster: Yes it is, Jed. Between 10 billion and 20 billion years ago, this incredibly small, heavy speck exploded. Its matter shot out with such force that it is still moving.

Out of this matter, the simplest elements in the universe formed, first hydrogen (HY druh juhn) and then helium (HEE lee uhm). All this happened within minutes after the big bang.

Hydrogen and helium gases filled the universe for 100 million years. Then gravity drew these gases into huge clouds. The clouds' gravity caused them to shrink, and they became smaller, denser clouds. Over a billion years, parts of these dense clouds formed stars and gave birth to the galaxies.

Big bang

Hydrogen and helium atoms

Gas-and-dust clouds

Early galaxies

Quasars

Distant galaxies

Nearby galaxies

Stars of the Milky Way

Magneti: You say that galaxies formed in only a billion years, Professor Aster? Sounds pretty unlikely to me. We know that our sun—one little star—took almost 5 billion years to develop. At that rate, galaxies would take 1 or 2 billion years to form, and galaxy superclusters would need at least a hundred billion years. Do you believe that galaxies developed very quickly for a billion years, then slowed down since then?

Aster: Yes. Galaxies indeed developed very quickly.

Magneti: Absurd!

Toppel: Professor Magneti, tell us how you think the universe began.

Magneti: Gladly, Jed. A Swedish scientist named Hannes Alfvén originated the plasma theory. Plasma (PLAZ muh) is electrically charged gas. Plasma exists in all the galaxies and sends out most radio signals from space.

In a laboratory, Alfvén observed threads of electrical currents in plasma. These threads formed a magnetic field that attracted other currents and plasma with them. These all gathered together to form strands of matter called *filaments* (FIHL uh muhnts). Electricity and magnetism caused matter to come together faster than

Electricity causes long strands of plasma, called filaments, to draw near each other, *below.*

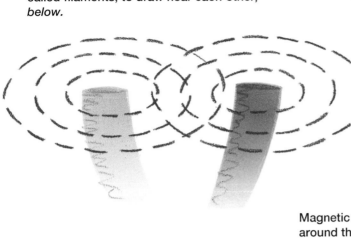

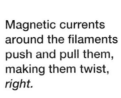

Magnetic currents around the filaments push and pull them, making them twist, *right.*

In space, clouds of plasma pull together just as filaments do. Their magnetic currents make them roll.

As the plasma clouds roll, they twist and pull into long, curved arms.

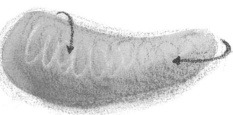

165

gravity could. Alfvén reasoned that if plasma works this way on Earth, it probably would act the same way in space.

Later, Tony Peratt, one of Alfvén's students, created whirlpools of filaments in the lab. Then Peratt designed a computer program to copy the same action on a bigger scale. The program resulted in whirlpools that matched the shape and radio waves of spiral galaxies in space.

Aster: If the galaxies began as plasma, how did the plasma begin?

Magneti: Perhaps plasma came from even simpler matter. I believe that the universe has been *evolving,* or changing, for a hundred billion years, at least—not a mere 10 or 20 billion—and that it will keep on evolving.

Aster: How do you explain the expanding universe? Do you deny that galaxies are moving ever outward?

Magneti: Many things besides the big bang could explain the movement of the galaxies.

The rolling arms are drawn toward each other, but their magnetic currents keep them from touching. The arms begin spinning around a magnetic center, and a new galaxy is born.

This photograph may show an early stage of a galaxy. The clusters of stars forming are at least 7 billion light-years away—some of the farthest stars ever seen.

Perhaps just our little corner of the universe experienced a big bang. It may have set in motion only the galaxies that we can observe.

Aster: Prove it!

Magneti: When you prove the big bang!

Toppel: Thank you, professors. And that's all the time we have. Tune in again next week, and remember what I always say: Feel free to disagree.

At the Edge of the Universe

Years ago, scientists thought they knew how big and how old the universe was. Then newly discovered objects in space proved these scientists wrong. Let's read about the discoveries that led scientists to believe that the universe is bigger and older than anyone imagined.

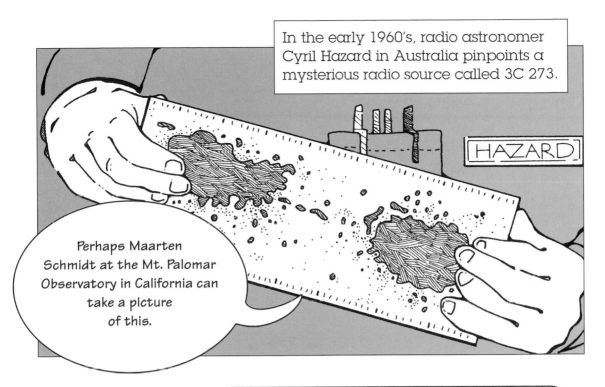

In the early 1960's, radio astronomer Cyril Hazard in Australia pinpoints a mysterious radio source called 3C 273.

Perhaps Maarten Schmidt at the Mt. Palomar Observatory in California can take a picture of this.

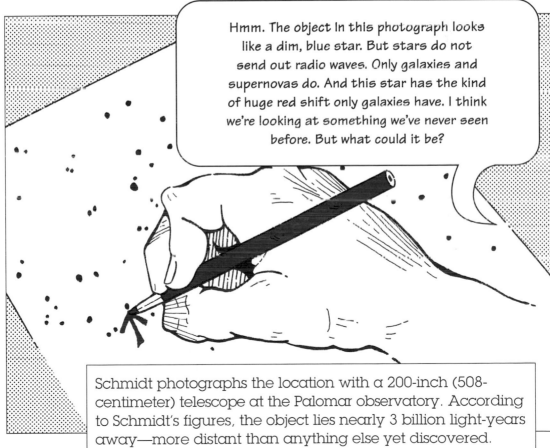

Hmm. The object in this photograph looks like a dim, blue star. But stars do not send out radio waves. Only galaxies and supernovas do. And this star has the kind of huge red shift only galaxies have. I think we're looking at something we've never seen before. But what could it be?

Schmidt photographs the location with a 200-inch (508-centimeter) telescope at the Palomar observatory. According to Schmidt's figures, the object lies nearly 3 billion light-years away—more distant than anything else yet discovered.

Schmidt calls coworker Jesse Greenstein into his office. Greenstein has photographed C3 48, a similar dim, blue star that does not act like a star.

Jesse, look at the red shift of this thing!

Wow. If that's right, C3 48 has a red shift more than twice as large. It must be 5 billion light-years away.

Other astronomers discover more and more of these distant objects. They call them *quasi-stellars* (which means "like stars"), or *quasars* for short.

We couldn't see mere stars at such great distances. These objects are much brighter than stars.

But they can't be galaxies. Galaxies would need thousands of years to change brightness across their whole width. These objects change brightness over months, weeks, and sometimes days.

They must be much smaller than galaxies. Yet each has the brightness of a thousand galaxies.

Then in 1965 ....

*Today, astronomers believe that the universe is between 10 billion and 20 billion years old.

In 1979, astronomers Susan Wyckoff and Peter Wehinger of Arizona use a special computer to study C3 273 in detail.

The Big Fade and the Big Crunch

Ms. Mendez, a third-grade science teacher, addressed her students: "Many astronomers believe that the universe will go on expanding forever. Others believe that matter in space will grow so heavy that its gravity. . . ."

"Blah, blah, blah," Yee-Kin mumbled to himself. "Science could be so much more fun. What this class needs is virtual reality helmets. Then we kids could travel into the universe of the future."

Yee-Kin leaned back in his chair. "I can picture it now. The solar system disappears from view on my virtual reality screens. I look up, I see stars. I look down, I see stars. I look to each side, I see more stars. I feel as though I'm jetting through space."

Ms. Mendez' words interrupted Yee-Kin's daydream. "It's possible that the universe may grow forever. Scientists call this kind of universe 'open.' "

"I wonder what an open universe will be like 1 trillion years from now?" Yee-Kin thought. "I'll program my virtual reality helmet to see for myself."

A ***virtual reality*** helmet takes you into a computer-made world. When you put on the helmet, you hear stereo sound and see three-dimensional images. To look around, you move your head. To "move about," you wear a special glove.

He whirled into the blackness. Space
seemed darker. The galaxies looked much
farther apart. Some stars had faded, and
Yee-Kin saw no new ones to replace them.
"Is the same thing going on in my own
solar system?" he wondered. With a
squeeze of his spaceball, he was back.
There was no good news: The sun had
shrunk to a dim dwarf!

Yee-Kin pushed on. "How will an open
universe look in 100 billion years? With a
touch of a button, I find out."

"Wow!" Yee-Kin breathed as he looked
at the scene. The planets had broken away
from their orbits. They floated through

space like tumbleweeds in the desert. Even the stars had drifted out of their galaxies. "The Milky Way looks more like a ghost town than a star city," Yee-Kin whispered to himself.

Yee-Kin fast-forwarded to peek at developments even farther in the future. The stars were gone. Black holes stalked the universe, gobbling all matter in their path. Yee-Kin kept fast-forwarding. He saw even the black holes breaking up. Like dying sparks, tiny bits of matter leaked out of the holes as they vanished.

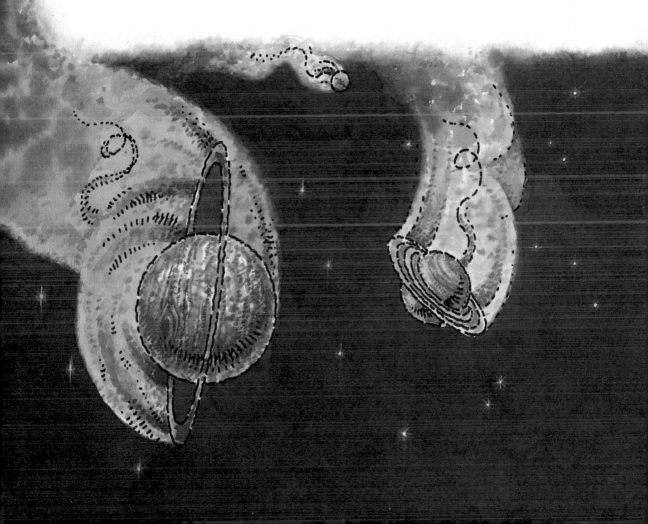

Finally, Yee-Kin found himself trillions of years in the future. "The only things left are the tiny particles in a vast, spreading blackness. Spooky!" he said to himself as he tuned back in to his teacher's lecture.

"Other scientists believe in a 'closed universe.'" said Ms. Mendez. "In this kind, gravity eventually stops the universe from growing."

"That's something! Time to see how that kind of universe will end up." Yee-Kin once again imagined himself in the future. After almost 50 billion years, supergiants had exploded and become black holes. Stars like the sun had ballooned into red giants

and then shrunk into white dwarfs. White dwarfs had turned into black dwarfs. Only red dwarfs seemed unchanged, burning with a dim glow.

As Yee-Kin fast-forwarded over several billion years, the galaxies appeared to move toward him. "Their gravity must be tugging them inward," he thought. The galaxies rushed together faster and faster.

Seventy billion years after the universe stopped growing, it has become blazingly bright. Trillions upon trillions of stars were crowded into a smaller and smaller space! "I can't look. It's too bright! Oh noooo!"

177

CRUNCH! The universe was no more.

"So that's what Ms. Mendez calls 'the big crunch,' " Yee-Kin thought. "The universe collapses into the smallest bit of matter possible. Later, this speck may explode and produce another universe."

"Yee-Kin?" Ms. Mendez says. "Explain a third theory that some scientists hold about the future of the universe."

"Huh?" Yee-Kin rubs his eyes. He is back from "inner space" and sitting at his desk.

Ms. Mendez frowns. "Well, let me explain for you. Some scientists believe that the universe will keep on expanding and evolving—creating new forms as old forms die out. According to these scientists, the universe will not run down or collapse. It will go on forever and ever."

Yee-Kin smiles and thinks, "Now that I would like to see. . . ."

Universe Watch

Things you need:
- two round balloons
- string
- marker
- measuring tape
- pencil and paper

Watching the red shift or blue shift of galaxies helps scientists understand how they move and how the universe changes. Here are two experiments that will help you see the same things.

The big bang

1. Use the marker to draw two small stars on one of the balloons: one near the neck, where you blow, and one at the other end.

2. Measure the distance between the two stars and write it down.

3. Blow up the balloon all the way. Have a grown-up or a friend tie it shut. Measure the distance between stars again and write it down. How did it change?

The big crunch

1. Blow up the second balloon all the way. Tie it shut or have a friend hold it shut.

2. With the marker, draw a star exactly opposite where you blow. Then measure outward 1 inch (2.5 centimeters) from the first star and draw another star.

1 inch

3. Repeat step 2 until you have a ring of six stars around the first star. This is your "galaxy." Measure the distance across your galaxy and write it down.

4. Now let the air out of the balloon. Measure the distance again. How did it change? How does your galaxy look now?

Living in the Space Age

"**B**oy, I hope I'm not around when the big crunch happens," said Annabelle when Major Vox finished his talk. "But how far *have* we gone, anyway?"

"That over there looks like a quasar," said Ben.

"But if that's a quasar, we're near the edge of the universe!" said Suki. "And that's far from home."

The children looked at each other and then at Major Vox. "It'll take us millions of years to get home," Annabelle cried.

Major Vox knew he had to do something quick. "That's it!" he exclaimed, grabbing a sock from under Little Rollo's seat.

"I'm sorry, Major Vox," cried Little Rollo. "I'll pick up my things. I promise."

"No, Little Rollo," he said with a laugh, "You've given me the answer. We'll use SpacePod's Magnetic Reorganizer to turn this wormhole inside out, like a sock. Then the white hole will become a black hole, and the black hole will become a white hole, and we'll end up where we started!"

Major Vox drew his eyes down close to his head, held his breath, and threw a switch. Two giant magnets sprang from under SpacePod's wings. Everything began to whirl and blur as the magnets drew the inside of the wormhole toward the ship. The kids hung on tight. To distract his worried travel companions, Major Vox began to tell them about living in the space age.

The Future Is Now

Science fiction is fun, but early science fiction can be funny, too. Years ago, books and movies often predicted futures that now seem light-years from real life.

But some artists, authors, and movie writers of long ago showed amazing abilities to predict what would really happen in the future. Look at this picture of a rocket ship from 1870, for example. It went along with a story by Jules Verne, who is known as the "father of science fiction." The rocket looks like the boosters that are used to lift spacecraft out of Earth's atmosphere. Did Verne predict the future, or did modern rocket designers get ideas from him?

A rocket ship in an 1870 illustration from a book by Jules Verne

The space shuttle Discovery with its modern rocket boosters

Here is an illustration from the H. G. Wells book *The First Men in the Moon*. It pictures the effects of weightlessness aboard a ship in space. Notice the pipe. Astronauts would never pollute the air in a spacecraft by smoking. What other items aboard Wells's ship would today's astronauts say "No way" to?

Astronauts in a 1901 illustration from a book by H. G. Wells

Compare reality with the artist's early fantasy. What effect of weightlessness did the artist for Wells's book overlook?

A weightless astronaut in a modern spacecraft

Skip ahead now to 1929. That was the year that the Germans made the science-fiction movie *The Woman in the Moon.* In this scene from the movie, Earth's satellite seems to have plenty of air and gravity.

The astronaut here looks much better prepared for actual conditions on the moon. He carries his air supply on his back and wears weights in his boots.

Astronauts strolling on the moon in a 1929 movie

Astronaut on an actual moonwalk in a full space suit

Flash Gordon, *center*, dressed for space in a 1930's movie

During the 1930's, people loved short movies starring Flash Gordon, space explorer. Here Flash and his crew face unfriendly aliens. His costume comes close to the casual clothing astronauts prefer when working aboard a spacecraft.

Modern astronaut at work in casual clothes

Two famous movie robots, C3PO, *left,* and R2D2, *right,* from *Star Wars*

The crew members of the Starship Enterprise always "boldly go where no one has gone before" in their uniforms. They never wear space suits that protect them from extreme temperatures and other dangers of space. Perhaps by the year 2500, space travelers will rub on some kind of protection the way we put on sun block. In the 1990's, however, astronauts always wear space suits when they leave their spacecraft.

C3PO, one of the *Star Wars* robots, resembles a slimmed-down version of today's space suit. But the most useful robot in space today is called the Canadarm— a 50-foot (15-meter), Canadian-made extension arm on American shuttles. Astronauts use it to launch and rescuc satellites. And it looks nothing like C3PO.

Will our future be anything like the latest science fiction? Maybe, maybe not. We will have to wait and see.

Science fiction or fact?

FICTION "Weightlessness occurs because there is no gravity."

Fact. There is gravity on a spacecraft, although it is a small fraction of the gravity on Earth. When a spacecraft's engines stop and the ship coasts through space, its motion cancels the pull of gravity. So weightlessness occurs.

Canadarm, a robot arm, mounted on a space shuttle

Getting By in Space

Welcome to the annual Space Settlers Convention. Each year we draw closer to our goal of building colonies in space. Today's panel from the National Aeronautics and Space Administration (NASA) includes the commander of a space shuttle, a doctor of medicine, and a professor of psychology. They are here to answer questions about travel and life in space.

Commander, while traveling in space, did you look any different?

Commander: Quite a bit. For instance, I grew 2 inches (5 centimeters). On Earth, gravity presses together a person's spine, or backbone. In weightlessness, the spine stretches. Weightlessness also gave me a temporary face-lift—but not a very good one. Without gravity, body fluids rise toward the upper half of the body. My face started to look puffy. After about three days in space, my body flushed out what it felt was extra fluid, and my face lost some of the puffiness.

Do people in space become dehydrated, or lose too much fluid from their bodies?

Doctor: Astronauts' bodies reach a level of fluid that is comfortable for them in weightlessness. This is a welcome sign for future space colonists. It shows that our bodies adapt to conditions in space.

By the way, weightlessness also causes astronauts' hearts to grow bigger at first. On long flights, their hearts get weaker because they don't have to pump against gravity. Scientists are trying to find out whether this would be a serious problem for astronauts on very long flights.

Astronauts often feel faint or dizzy when they return to Earth. After a few weeks, their bodies readjust to gravity. They regain body fluid and their hearts go back to normal.

Can weightlessness cause health problems?

Doctor: Astronauts who spend months rather than days in weightlessness lose strength in their bones and leg muscles. Their muscles grow weak because they don't use them. Space shuttle crews work out on treadmills and exercise cycles to slow this weakening of bones and muscles. Crews on a space station probably would have to do the same. It is possible that scientists could develop some kind of "artificial gravity" for space stations, too.

Weightlessness also decreases the number of certain kinds of cells in the blood. This loss can be deadly if an astronaut gets a bad cut. Space shuttle scientists study blood cell loss in rats to find out more about this problem in humans.

190

Special instruments measure the energy used on a weightless "run" in space, *left.*

Which way is up? An astronaut spins in a chair while instruments measure her reactions to motion, *left.*

An exercise bike gives astronauts a chance to work out on long trips aboard a space shuttle, *above.*

Pictures show how an ACRV would return to Earth from a disabled spacecraft, *left*, and land with the aid of parachutes, *above*.

What would happen if an astronaut were to get seriously ill or injured on a mission in space?

Commander: In case of an emergency on the shuttle, we would return to Earth immediately. In the future, emergencies will be handled differently, however. Engineers plan to include an Assured Crew Return Vehicle (ACRV). This craft acts like a lifeboat on a ship. An ill or injured crew member could be taken to Earth aboard an ACRV.

Of course, the space station would have a doctor on its crew. But he or she will not be able to handle all emergencies. Perhaps someday, a surgeon on Earth may use virtual reality to control a robot operating on a patient in space.

Will astronauts ever learn how to grow food successfully in space?

A **space station** is a large human-made satellite placed in orbit around Earth. Its functions may include acting as a base for research and as a launch site for spacecraft. NASA hopes to work with many other countries to build a space station by the year 2000.

Commander: Yes, one day astronauts may raise their own food in space. Skylab and shuttle crews have experimented with growing rice, beans, and oats. These plants grow in space, but some of their roots grow up out of the soil in weightlessness.

A special wick in this "salad machine" holds down the roots of lettuce growing in weightlessness.

Does living in space change the way people think or the way they view life?

Professor: Astronauts have often said that they think differently about time while in space. After all, in the shuttle's orbit, the time between sunrise and sunset is only about 45 minutes. In outer space, the length of daylight changes from planet to planet. There are no days as we know them on Earth.

Also, many astronauts say that from space they cannot see the borders that divide countries. Of course, they did not expect to. But viewing Earth from afar makes you realize that all humans travel through space on the same "ship," the planet Earth.

Some astronauts look at gravity in a new way. They say weightlessness feels so natural. Sally Ride, the first U.S. woman in space, says that "it feels wonderful to be able to float without effort; to slither up, down, and around the inside of the shuttle just like a seal; to be upside down as often as I'm right side up and have it make no difference."

Africa, the Arabian Peninsula, and parts of two oceans show through the clouds in this photo of Earth from space.

Thank you, panelists. You have given us a lot to consider. Of course, only we can answer our last and most important question: Should we or should we not colonize space?

Explore the Effects of Weightlessness

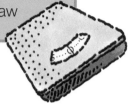

1. Ask a grown-up you know to do this experiment with you. Bring a scale into an elevator. Use an elevator that is not too busy.

2. Stand on the scale. Check your normal weight before you push a button.

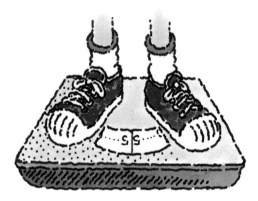

3. Push a button for an upper floor. Check the scale as the elevator starts. It should show more than your normal weight, because gravity pulls you down as the elevator moves up.

4. Check the scale as the elevator stops. The reading should be less than your normal weight, because your body is still trying to move up. It's pushing against gravity and canceling its force.

5. Try the experiment as the elevator goes down. What happens to your weight?

Not only are astronauts weightless in space, but so is everything else, including their food and drink. How does this affect life aboard a spacecraft? Try this experiment and see.

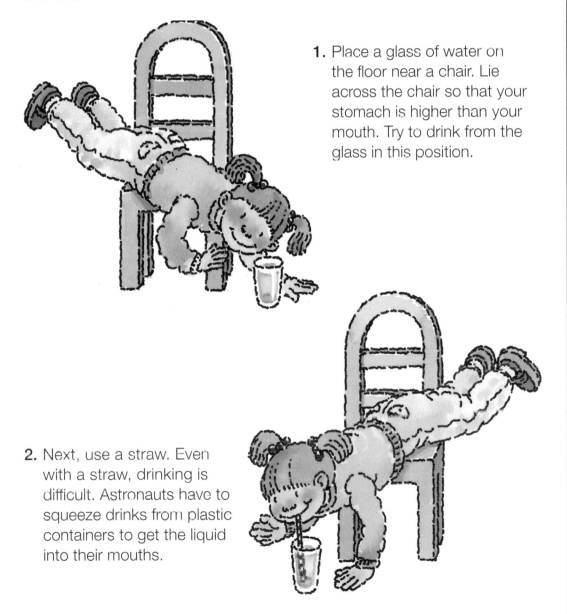

1. Place a glass of water on the floor near a chair. Lie across the chair so that your stomach is higher than your mouth. Try to drink from the glass in this position.

2. Next, use a straw. Even with a straw, drinking is difficult. Astronauts have to squeeze drinks from plastic containers to get the liquid into their mouths.

Really Fast Food

The **payload** on a spacecraft includes the people, scientific instruments, and other things directly related to the purpose of the flight. It does not include the things needed to fly the spacecraft.

Maria, the payload commander on the space shuttle, has spent her morning hours observing how rats adapt to weightlessness. Now she is ready for lunch. In the galley, she grabs a tray and sticks a spoon, a fork, and a knife to the magnets on the side of the tray. Otherwise, her tableware would float away. She also takes a pair of scissors. She'll need them to open food packets.

"Hmmm," Maria thinks. "What looks good today?" The crew can choose from more than 100 different foods and drinks.

Maria has no trouble deciding on a tortilla. Tortillas are the only kind of bread the shuttle has. Other kinds dry out too quickly in the shuttle. They also make crumbs, which float around the cabin.

Next, she selects a container of milk, a can of chicken salad, and a plastic packet of dried apricots. She wedges them into slots on her tray. She prefers her chicken salad warm, so she places it in a special kind of oven to heat it.

"This chicken salad can taste pretty bland," Maria recalls. So she picks up packets of liquid salt and pepper. If the shuttle crew used regular salt and pepper, the grains would float about. That could cause a lot of sneezing.

"Maria, hand me some hot sauce, will you, please?" Rick, the pilot, asks. Maria remembers that Rick avoided spicy foods during training back on Earth. But in space, he cannot seem to put enough hot sauce on his food.

In microgravity, body fluids rise toward the head and stop up noses. Maria thinks this dulls the crew members' sense of taste and smell. So they use plenty of pepper, salt, and such condiments as hot sauce and ketchup on their food to add flavor.

Microgravity describes gravity conditions aboard a spacecraft. Despite the state of weightlessness, gravity still exists even though its pull equals a small fraction of gravity's pull on Earth.

Maria slips her feet into straps on the floor. She does not need a seat to hold up her body. Microgravity takes care of that. She straps her tray to her leg and digs in.

She can spread chicken salad on her tortilla as easily as on Earth. Foods like chicken salad and thick soup stick to knives and spoons in space. But they may fly off and up if she were to fling her hand or make some other sudden movement.

Drinking requires more care. Maria squeezes her container as she sips milk from a straw. She stops drinking but keeps pressing, and a drop of milk escapes. It loooks like a white bubble suspended in front of her nose.

Maria lunges forward and captures the bubble in her mouth. Rick laughs. He does not notice the red berry drink rising out of his straw. Now Rick is the one chasing bubbles, and Maria gets the last laugh.

A Star in Space

Mae Jemison

Dr. Mae Jemison believes young students like science, but they lose their interest as they get older. She thinks it's because they get the wrong message. They hear that studying and enjoying science are not "in" things to do.

Dr. Jemison's adventures as an astronaut prove just how "far out" a scientist can get. On September 12, 1992, she rocketed into orbit as science mission specialist aboard the shuttle Endeavour. And she became the very first African-American woman to make the journey into space.

According to Jemison, the space program should include

Mae Jemison, science mission specialist

Mae Jemison in flight, on a joint mission of the United States and Japan

all kinds of people. She strongly encourages minorities and girls to study math and science. Then they too can be astronauts or, at least, better understand how discoveries made in space affect their everyday lives.

Jemison says that space research pays off by creating new types of businesses and jobs. Recently, she started a company to develop a satellite communications system.

Other companies also make products that began with space gadgets. For example, the cordless vacuum cleaner is a spin-off from the special drill used to pull up moon rocks. And some walking shoes are made of the same shock-absorbing material that helped to lighten the steps of astronauts in space. And the list goes on and on.

Does Dr. Jemison have other interests besides science? "I had all kinds of music in space," she says. "Stevie Wonder, Olatunji, Hiroshima, Aretha Franklin, and Nancy Wilson. . . . I was jammin'." It just goes to show that scientists can enjoy a good time, even aboard the space shuttle.

UFO's and Close Encounters

Extra! Extra! Read all about it. People all over the globe have spotted unidentified flying objects (UFO's). Find out what aliens do to unsuspecting Earthlings. Then judge for yourself— are these true stories or are people's imaginations working overtime?

The military claimed that these fragments of a weather balloon were mistakenly identified as a crashed flying saucer.

July 8, 1947

Flying Disc Crashes— Or Does It?

ROSWELL, New Mexico—United States Army Lieutenant Walter Haut announces that the Army has recovered a crashed "flying disc." But later the same day, the Army claims that the earlier story was a mistake—the remains were really pieces of a weather balloon. The U.S. government has stood by the second story ever since.

We may never know what really happened. Witnesses, including ranchers and Army officers, reported that the wreckage looked like "nothing from this Earth." They described flexible beams with mysterious symbols on them; paper-thin metal that couldn't be dented, cut, or burned; and foil that smoothed itself out automatically when crumpled.

Some witnesses also claimed they saw bodies of the alien crew. They described the bodies as 3 or 4 feet (about 1 meter) tall, with big heads, large eyes, and thin arms and legs. Even today, some people claim that the bodies are preserved in a secret location.

June 12, 1950

Farmer Snaps Saucer

McMINNVILLE, Oregon—On May 11 at 7:30 p.m., Paul Trent heard his wife call out. When he rushed outside, he saw what looked like a huge metal dish floating overhead. His wife had already fetched a camera and urged him to take pictures. As Trent snapped the airborne object twice, it sped into the western sky. The Trents' pictures are the first clear photos of a UFO.

A photo taken by Paul Trent showed this object flying overhead.

December 29, 1957

Aliens Capture Young Man

BRASÍLIA, Brazil—Earlier this year, farmer Antonio Villas Boas was plowing his field when he saw an egg-shaped craft land just ahead of him. The engine on Boas' tractor suddenly died. Then four humanlike creatures seized the young man and dragged him into their spacecraft. There they took a sample of blood from Boas' chin and placed him back in the field before dawn. Later, a doctor's examination revealed two odd scars on Boas' chin.

A **UFO** is an "unidentified flying object." The term refers to an unexplained object flying in the sky or touching down on Earth. It need not be a ship from space. A United States Air Force officer came up with the term in the early 1950's.

June 28, 1959

Saucer Signals Priest

PAPUA, New Guinea—On June 26 at 6:45 p.m., priest William Gill and more than 30 other witnesses watched four "men" emerge from a sparkling disc hovering overhead. According to Father Gill, the figures were lit "by this curious halo. . . ." The next night, the disc and men returned. Gill waved at the creatures, and to his surprise, the aliens waved back. Then Gill signaled with a flashlight. In response, the saucer swung back and forth several times.

A color photo of the place where Ronald Johnson says he saw a hovering object shows a round spot with a ring of crusted soil.

November 2, 1971

Glowing Object Lands in Kansas

DELPHOS, Kansas—Sixteen-year-old Ronald Johnson was doing his evening farm chores when he heard an unusual rumbling noise. He looked up to see a red-orange-and-blue glowing object hovering near the ground a short distance away. The object was about 9 feet (2.7 meters) across and 10 feet (3 meters) tall. He watched as the object began to rise. With a noise like a jet plane, it sailed over the farm buildings. The glow was so bright that Ronald was temporarily blinded. When Ronald's sight returned, he called his parents. The three watched as the object disappeared into the southern sky. Then they examined the spot where the object had hovered. The dirt glowed in the dark, and it had turned grayish-white and crusty as though it had melted. When Mrs. Johnson touched the dirt, she felt numbness in her fingertips that lasted about two weeks. The Johnsons reported what they saw, and several people photographed the spot.

June 23, 1978

Close Encounter Revealed

AVELEY, England—One night in 1974, the Avis family was driving on a lonely road when a green mist surrounded the car and jolted it. After arriving home, none of the family members could remember what they did during three hours of their trip. A few years later under *hypnosis* (deep relaxation), they told how 4-foot (101.5-centimeter) aliens forced them aboard a spaceship and performed medical examinations on them.

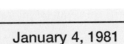

January 4, 1981

Diamond in the Sky

HOUSTON, Texas—Soon after Christmas, Betty Cash, Vickie Landrum, and Landrum's seven-year-old grandson, Colby, were riding home on a deserted road. A bright, diamond-shaped object appeared above the pines and floated toward them. The women left their car for a better look, although Landrum quickly returned to comfort Colby. The object's great heat forced Cash back into the car. Then about 20 large helicopters roared into the sky and sped away with the object. All three witnesses developed blisters on their skin that looked like radiation burns.

Author J. Allen Hynek described three kinds of up-close UFO sightings. A **close encounter of the first kind** is a sighting within 500 feet (155 meters) of the UFO. A **close encounter of the second kind** is a sighting of a UFO plus some effect the UFO causes, such as a stalled car engine. A **close encounter of the third kind** is a sighting that includes living beings as well as the flying object.

Sept. 27, 1989

Teen Vanishes Under Alien Spell

VORONEZH, Soviet Union—At 6:30 p.m., while playing in a park, students Genya Blinov, Vasya Surin, and Julia Sholokhova say they saw a strange pink light in the sky. Soon the light turned dark red and round. It circled about forty feet above the ground, blowing the grass below, then zipped away. The UFO returned after a few minutes, and a crowd gathered.

These witnesses report that an alien 10 feet (3 meters) tall came out of the UFO. It was dressed in silver clothing and bronze boots and seemed to have three eyes. Next to it was a thing that looked like a robot. The alien made the robot move by touching it, and a boy screamed in fright. The alien stared at the boy, freezing him in place, then vanished. The UFO reappeared five minutes later. This time, the alien pointed a long tube at a 16-year-old boy, who quickly disappeared. The UFO flew away, and as the round light traveled through the sky, the teenager reappeared.

Is Time Travel Possible?

My friends call me Future Man because I think about the future a lot. Actually, I think about how to get to the future. And I wouldn't mind visiting the past, either.

Of course, we all travel into the future. In just one second, for instance, you will have traveled to the end of this sentence. However, this is not as exciting as traveling to the past or far-distant future.

Many people doubt that humans ever have traveled or ever will travel through time. Otherwise, they say, we would have met these time travelers, and we have not. But is this true? People have reported ghosts and UFO's. Might ghosts be time travelers from the past? Or might UFO's carry visitors from the future?

To understand one way to travel through time, go back with me to the early 1900's. Until then, people thought time flowed at a steady rate everywhere in the universe. A German-born American scientist named Albert Einstein changed their thinking. He showed that time slows down for objects traveling at great speeds.

Einstein claimed that objects have to travel close to the speed of light to slow down any noticeable amount. The astronauts who went to the moon, for instance, reached a top speed of 24,300 miles (40,225 kilometers) an hour. Light

Albert Einstein

Leave Earth in 1994

Return to Earth hundreds of years later

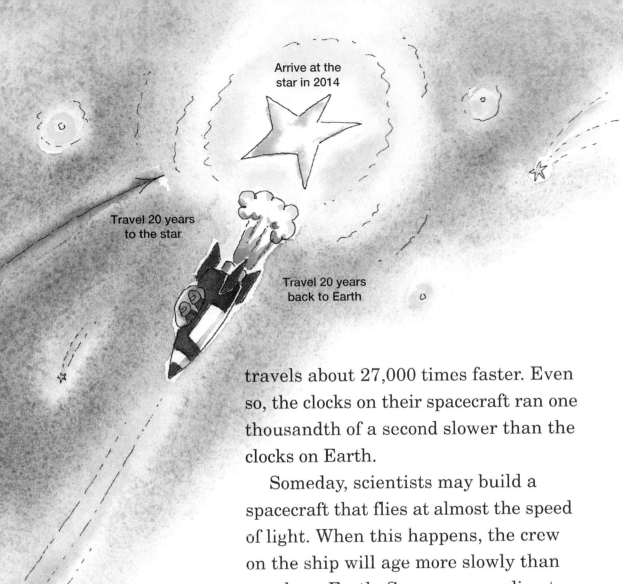

Arrive at the
star in 2014

Travel 20 years
to the star

Travel 20 years
back to Earth

travels about 27,000 times faster. Even so, the clocks on their spacecraft ran one thousandth of a second slower than the clocks on Earth.

Someday, scientists may build a spacecraft that flies at almost the speed of light. When this happens, the crew on the ship will age more slowly than people on Earth. Suppose, according to the clock on this ship, the crew journeys 20 years to a star and 20 years back. On their return, hundreds of years will have passed on Earth.

This crew will have traveled far into the future. So spaceships that approach the speed of light may be one kind of time machine. But few people would choose to leave behind the world they know and to return to a totally different place.

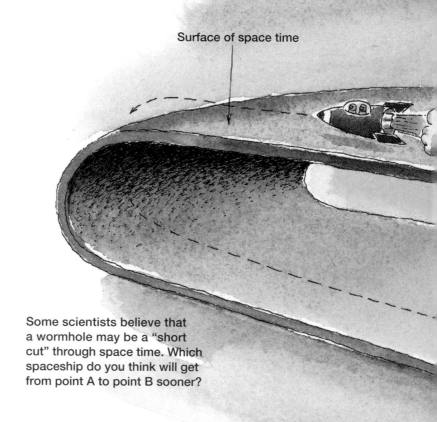

Surface of space time

Some scientists believe that a wormhole may be a "short cut" through space time. Which spaceship do you think will get from point A to point B sooner?

Another form of time travel involves black holes. Some scientists believe that black holes open into tunnels called *wormholes*. Wormholes are thought to be short cuts in place and time. They lead to exits called *white holes*. If a spacecraft entered a black hole, traveled through the wormhole, and came out a white hole, it might find itself in the past or far-distant future.

Major obstacles stand in the way of this form of time travel. First, black holes may not even exist. Second, if black holes do exist, their strong gravity probably tears

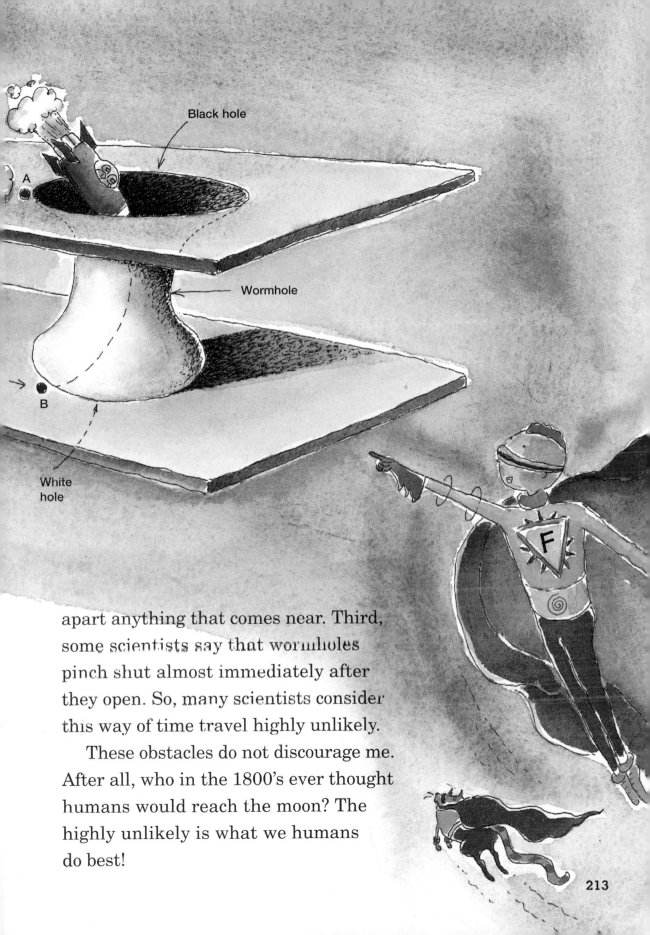

Black hole

Wormhole

White
hole

A

B

F

apart anything that comes near. Third,
some scientists say that wormholes
pinch shut almost immediately after
they open. So, many scientists consider
this way of time travel highly unlikely.

These obstacles do not discourage me.
After all, who in the 1800's ever thought
humans would reach the moon? The
highly unlikely is what we humans
do best!

The Crew Heads Home

SpacePod's magnets dragged the white hole through the wormhole. "I think it's working," said Major Vox. "We'll be out of here in no time."

"Hey, there's another SpacePod!" cried Little Rollo. "And the crew looks just like us."

"Jumpin' Jupiters! That *is* us," said Major Vox.

They all looked in wonder at the other SpacePod as their "twins" looked back at them.

"By turning the wormhole inside out, we've turned time topsy turvy," said Major Vox. "We're meeting ourselves as we were hours ago when we first went into the wormhole."

"Look out!" cried Little Rollo.

They were about to crash into the SpacePod of the past. "Abandon ship!" Major Vox yelled.

A furious rattling dumped the crew out of their seats, and they felt the ship spinning and spinning in space. A cloud of rainbow colors boiled around both SpacePods. The whole crew, even Major Vox, screamed in fright. Then the noise and tumbling stopped, and they heard a small click. The two SpacePods had merged. The crew was safe in their seats.

"Is everyone okay?" asked Major Vox as he checked his instruments. "It looks like the ship's clock stopped in all that ruckus. What time is it?"

Everyone's watch said 12:30—the time they had entered the black hole.

"But that's not possible. We were gone for hours," said Ben.

"Yeah, what happened to all that time?" Little Rollo asked. "If it didn't pass, how can we remember it?"

"That's a question not even I can answer," Major Vox replied. "Space time remains one of the deep mysteries of the universe. Maybe one of you will solve it someday. Right, Little Rollo?"

But Little Rollo didn't hear. He was fast asleep, wearing a smile as peaceful as a starry night.

Books to Read

Check your school or public library for more books about space and space exploration. Here are some titles you may enjoy:

Ages 5-8

Astronaut to Zodiac
by Roger Ressmeyer (Crown, 1992)
★ This unique alphabet book captures the adventure of space through dramatic photographs.

The Big Dipper
by Franklyn M. Branley (HarperCollins Publishers, 1991)
★ Which stars make up the Big Dipper? How does its position in the sky change? This book answers these questions and more. You may also enjoy *Journey into a Black Hole* and *What the Moon Is Like* by the same author.

How We Learned the Earth Is Round
by Patricia Lauber (Crowell, 1990)
★ Read about how our beliefs about the shape of Earth have changed over the years. Colorful, cartoonlike illustrations help explain.

The Magic School Bus Lost in the Solar System
by Joanna Cole (Scholastic, 1990)
★ Ms. Frizzle and her class find the planetarium closed for repairs, so they take a trip to the real solar system. Join them as they explore the moon, the planets, and the sun.

My Place in Space
by Robin Hirst (Orchard Books, 1990)
★ Just where do Henry Wilson and his sister live in relation to the rest of the universe? Find out in this wonderfully illustrated book.

So That's How the Moon Changes Shape
by Allan Fowler (Children's Press, 1991)
★ This fun book gives a simple explanation of the moon and why it changes shape day by day.

Star Gazers
by Gail Gibbons (Holiday House, 1992)
★ Here are the answers to your basic questions about the stars, including how constellations were named and how a telescope works.

The Starry Sky
by Rose Wyler (Messner, 1989)
★ Learn all about day and night, the moon's phases, the stars, and the planets. Fun, simple experiments help you to better understand how the solar system works.

Which Way to the Milky Way?
by Sidney Rosen (Carolrhoda Books, 1992)
★ Cartoon characters are your guides to fun and excitement as you explore the dazzling center of the Milky Way and map distant galaxies. Also by the same author: *Where Does the Moon Go?*

Ages 8-12

Astronomy
by Carol J. Amato (Smithmark, 1992)

★ With stunning photographs, this book explores the many fascinating and important discoveries that have been made about the universe.

The Constellations: How They Came to Be
by Roy A. Gallant (Four Winds Press, 1991)

★ Learn how to "read" the night sky at different times of the year. Careful illustrations and photos help explain the backgrounds of each constellation.

Exploring the Sky: 100 Projects for Beginning Astronomers
by Richard Moeschl (Chicago Review, 1989)

★ This information-packed book will keep you exploring space for hours.

The Great Voyager Adventure: A Guided Tour Through the Solar System
by Alan Harris (Messner, 1990)

★ This lively book discusses the Voyager space probes and what they have revealed about Jupiter, Saturn, Uranus, and Neptune.

Janice VanCleave's Gravity
by Janice VanCleave (Wiley, 1993)

★ See for yourself how gravity works with this fun-filled book of experiments.

Mythology and the Universe
by Issac Asimov (G. Stevens, 1990)

★ Astrology, constellations, and superstitious beliefs about comets and eclipses are all discussed in this nicely illustrated book. Other books by this same author include *How Did We Find Out About Neptune?, Pluto: A Double Planet?,* and *Comets and Meteors.*

Rand McNally Children's Atlas of the Universe
(Rand McNally, 1990)

★ Travel throughout the universe with this exceptional book as your guide. You'll learn about Earth, the other objects in our solar system, and the Milky Way and other galaxies.

Small Worlds: Exploring the 60 Moons of Our Solar System
by Joseph Kelch (Messner, 1990)

★ This exciting and information-packed book tells of the origin and characteristics of each of the moons circling the planets of the solar system.

Superstar: The Supernova of 1987
by Franklyn M. Branley (Crowell, 1990)

★ The author explains the nature and origin of supernovas, the information they provide about the formation of stars and planets, and what we learned from Supernova 1987A. Striking photos show off the beauty of supernovas.

The Sun
by Michael George (Creative Education, 1991)

★ Beautiful photographs show the many characteristics of the sun, including sunspots, flares, and eclipses.

New Words

Here are some words you have read in this book, mainly those that don't appear in the margin with a symbol near them. Some of them may be new to you. Next to each word you'll see how to say the word: **constellation** (KAHN stuh LAY shuhn). Say the part in large capital letters louder than the rest of the word, and the part in small capital letters a little louder. One or two sentences tell the word's meaning as it is used in this book.

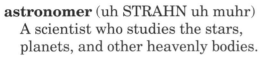

astronomer (uh STRAHN uh muhr) A scientist who studies the stars, planets, and other heavenly bodies.

atmosphere (AT muh sfeer) The mixture of gases that surrounds a heavenly body.

aurora (aw RAWR uh) Bands of light that appear in the night sky, especially around the poles. Auroras are caused when electrically charged bits of matter collide.

big bang (bihg bang) The theory that the universe began as a big explosion.

big crunch (bihg kruhnch) The theory that many, many years from now the universe will collapse into a very small, heavy bit of matter.

black hole (blak hohl) A collapsed star or other object whose gravity is so strong that nothing, including light, can escape from it.

coaccretion (COH uh KREE shun) One theory of how the moon began, which says that matter in space came together to form the moon.

collision (kuh LIHZH uhn) One theory of how the Earth's moon began, which says that an object crashed into Earth, knocking off a piece of material that eventually became the moon.

constellation (KAHN stuh LAY shuhn) A group of stars that forms a picture of a person, animal, or some other thing.

corona (kuh ROH nuh) A ring of light that can be seen around the sun and some other heavenly bodies. It is caused by dust and fiery gas.

Earthday (urthday) The time it takes Earth to rotate around the sun, equal to about 24 hours.

eclipse (ih KLIHPS) A total or partial blocking of light when one heavenly body passes into the shadow of another.

fission (FIHSH uhn) One theory of how the moon began, which says that the moon may have split off from Earth.

flare (flair) A huge explosion that occurs in areas around sunspots on the surface of the sun. Flares can interfere with radio waves and electric power all over the world.

gravity (GRAV uh tee) The force that pulls objects toward the earth, sun, or other heavenly bodies.

light-year (lyt yeer) The distance light travels in one year, equal to 5,880,000,000,000 miles (9,460,000,000,000 kilometers).

magnetosphere (mag NEE tuh sfeer) An area around Earth and other planets that works like a magnet to pull in certain bits of matter from outer space. The magnetosphere shields the Earth from harmful bits of matter.

maria (MAHR ee uh) Dark areas of rock on the surface of the moon.

mass (mas) The amount of matter something contains.

Milky Way (MIHL kee way) One of billions of galaxies, or groups of stars, in the universe. The sun, Earth, and the other planets around the sun are part of the Milky Way.

momentum (moh MEHN tuhm) The force with which an object moves. A heavy, fast-moving object has more momentum than a lighter, slower-moving one.

neutron star (NOO trahn stahr) A heavenly body that is made up of densely packed particles probably resulting from the collapse of a large star.

nova (NOH vuh) A star that suddenly becomes thousands of times brighter and then becomes dim again.

orbital capture (AWR buh tuhl KAP chuhr) One theory of how the moon began, which says that the moon came from somewhere far away in the solar system and was captured by Earth's gravity.

orbiter (AWR biht uhr) A spacecraft with scientific instruments that circles planets, making observations and sending them back to Earth.

pulsar (PUHL sahr) A tiny star that sends off short bursts of radio waves.

quasar (KWAY zahr) One of many heavenly bodies that are larger than stars but smaller than galaxies and send off very powerful light and radio waves. Scientists think quasars are the centers of extremely distant galaxies.

regolith (REHG uh lihth) A deep layer of dust that covers the surface of the moon.

satellite (SAT uh lyt) Also known as a moon. A heavenly body that rotates around a planet. An artificial satellite is a device sent up by people to take scientific measurements.

solar wind (SOH luhr wihnd) Tiny, electrically charged bits of matter that stream out from the sun in all directions.

space probe (spays prohb) A spacecraft that carries scientific instruments to make observations in space and record information or report it back to Earth.

star cluster (stahr CLUHS tuhr) A group of stars that are fairly close together.

sunspot (SUHN spaht) Cooler areas on the sun that appear as dark areas.

supernova (soo puhr NOH vuh) A star that explodes and then becomes billions of times brighter for a few weeks.

tide (tyd) The rise and fall of the level of the ocean, which usually takes place about every 12 hours and is caused by the gravitational pull of the moon and the sun.

white dwarf (wyt dworf) A small, white star with a large amount of material packed into a very small space.

white hole (wyt hohl) A hole in outer space where some scientists believe matter and energy leave a black hole.

wormhole (WUHRM hohl) The tunnel through which some scientists believe an object travels after it enters a black hole.

Illustration Acknowledgments

The publishers of *Childcraft* gratefully acknowledge the courtesy of the following illustrators, photographers, agencies, and organizations for illustrations in this volume. When all the illustrations for a sequence of pages are from a single source, the inclusive page numbers are given. Credits should be read from left to right, top to bottom, on their respective pages. All illustrations are the exclusive property of the publishers of *Childcraft* unless names are marked with an asterisk (*).

Cover:	Aristocrat, Standard, and Discovery Bindings—Roberta Polfus Heritage Binding—Roberta Polfus; © 1992 Roger Ressmeyer, Starlight*; Roberta Polfus; Jared D. Lee; Roberta Polfus; Roberta Polfus; Roberta Polfus; NASA*; NASA*
1	Randy Verougstraete
2-3	Roberta Polfus
4-5	Steven D. Mach; Daniel Powers
6-7	Patti Boyd; Eileen Mueller Neill; Steven D. Mach
8-9	Carl Whiting
10-11	Roberta Polfus and Carl Whiting
12-13	Jared D. Lee
14-15	NASA*; Jared D. Lee; NASA*; Jared D. Lee
16-17	Jared D. Lee; NASA*; Jared D. Lee; NASA*
18-19	Jared D. Lee; NASA*; John Sandford
20-21	John Sandford
22-27	Joe Van Severen
28-29	Susan Schmidt; NASA*
30-31	NASA*; NASA*; NASA*; Susan Schmidt
32-35	Steven D. Mach
36-39	Marilyn Mets
40-41	John Sandford
42-43	NASA*; Don Dixon
44-45	Lowell Observatory*
46-47	Roberta Polfus and Carl Whiting
48-51	Patti Boyd
52-53	Daniel Powers
54-55	NASA*; Daniel Powers; NASA*; NASA*; Daniel Powers
56-57	Daniel Powers
58-59	Daniel Powers; John Sandford
60-61	Lane Yerkes; NASA*; NASA*
62-63	Lane Yerkes; NASA*
64-69	Lane Yerkes
70-73	Jared D. Lee
74-75	Jared D. Lee; European Southern Observatory*; Jared D. Lee
76-77	Maria Mitchell Association*
78-79	George Ulrich; NASA*
80-81	George Ulrich
82-83	Steven D. Mach
84-85	Joe Van Severen; Arizona Department of Tourism*
86-87	Smithsonian Institution*; Sovfoto*
88-89	Joe Van Severen; John Sandford
90-91	Roberta Polfus and Carl Whiting
92-93	Susan Schmidt; U.S. Naval Research Laboratory*; Sacramento Peak Observatory*
96-97	Lydia Halverson
98-99	Lydia Halverson; © 1991 Roger Ressmeyer, Starlight*
100-101	© 1991 Roger Ressmeyer, Starlight*; Ken Sakamoto*; Lydia Halverson
102-103	Patti Boyd; National Optical Astronomy Observatories*; Granger Collection*; Patti Boyd
104-105	NASA*; Patti Boyd
106-107	John Sandford
108-109	Lane Yerkes; NASA*; Lane Yerkes
110-113	Allan Eitzen
114-115	Granger Collection*; Jay M. Pasachoff*
116-117	Hal Just
118-119	Roberta Polfus and Carl Whiting
120-121	Eileen Mueller Neill
122-123	Eileen Mueller Neill; Robert C. Mitchell*
124-125	John Sandford
126-127	Joan Holub; Anne Norica
128-129	National Optical Astronomy Observatories*; Joan Holub
130-131	Anglo-Australian Observatory*
132-133	National Optical Astronomy Observatories*; Herb Herrick
134-139	Daniel Powers
140-141	Randy Verougstraete; Space Telescope Science Institute Randy Verougstraete
142-143	Randy Verougstraete
144-145	Randy Verougstraete; National Optical Astronomy Observatories*; Randy Verougstraete
146-147	Frank L. Warren, TRW after NASA illustration*; Joe Van Severen
148-149	Joe Van Severen; AP/Wide World*
150-151	Roberta Polfus and Carl Whiting
152-153	Eileen Mueller Neill; U.S. Forest Service*
154-155	Eileen Mueller Neill; Robert Frerck, Odyssey Productions*
156-157	Randy Chewning
158-159	Randy Chewning; NASA*
160-161	J. R. Eyerman, *Life* Magazine © 1950 Time, Inc.*
162-165	Donna Kae Nelson
166-167	Space Telescope Science Institute*; Donna Kae Nelson
168-169	Carol Brozman
170-171	Carol Brozman; X-Ray Astronomy Group, Leicester University from Science Photo Library*
173-179	John Sandford
180-181	Roberta Polfus and Carl Whiting
182-183	From *From the Earth to the Moon* by Jules Verne, 1870*; NASA*; From *First Men on the Moon* by H. G. Wells, 1901*; NASA*
184-185	Film Stills Archive, Museum of Modern Art*; NASA*; Film Stills Archive, Museum of Modern Art*; NASA*
186-187	Lucasfilm, Ltd.*; NASA*
188-189	Lane Yerkes
190-191	Lane Yerkes; NASA*; NASA*
192-193	NASA*; Lane Yerkes; Lane Yerkes; NASA*
194-195	Lane Yerkes
196-197	John Sandford
198-201	Randy Verougstraete
202-203	NASA*
204-205	UPI/Bettmann*; Paul Trent, Mutual UFO Network*
206-207	Walter Andrus, Mutual UFO Network*; George Ulrich
208-209	George Ulrich; Steven D. Mach
210-211	AP/Wide World*; Steven D. Mach
212-213	Steven D. Mach
214-217	Carl Whiting
218-219	Steven D. Mach
220-221	Carl Whiting

Index

This index is an alphabetical list of the important topics covered in this book. It will help you find information given in both words and pictures. To help you understand what an entry means, there is sometimes a helping word in parentheses, for example, **Jupiter** (planet). If there is information in both words and pictures, you will see the words *with pictures* in parentheses after the page number. If there is only a picture, you will see the word *picture* in parentheses after the page number.

World Book Encyclopedia, Inc. provides high quality educational and reference products for the family and school, including a FIVE-VOLUME CHILDCRAFT FAVORITES SET, colorful books on favorite topics, such as DOGS and INDIANS; and THE WORLD BOOK/RUSH-PRESBYTERIAN-ST. LUKE'S MEDICAL CENTER MEDICAL ENCYCLOPEDIA, a 1,072-page, fully illustrated family health reference. For further information, write WORLD BOOK ENCYCLOPEDIA, INC., P.O. Box 3073, Evanston, IL 60204-3073.